# COOKING AND
# CANNING WITH
# MAMMA
# D'AMATO

# COOKING AND CANNING WITH MAMMA D'AMATO

## ANTOINETTE D'AMATO

WITH A FOREWORD BY

### Senator Alfonse D'Amato

ReganBooks

*An Imprint of HarperCollinsPublishers*

Frontispiece photograph courtesy of Ronald L. Glassman. All other photographs courtesy of the author.

FIRST EDITION

*Designed by Alma Hochhauser Orenstein*

Library of Congress Cataloging-in-Publication Data

D'Amato, Antoinette
     Cooking and canning with mamma D'Amato / by Antoinette D'Amato; with a foreword by Alfonse D'Amato.— 1st ed.
          p.     cm.
     Includes index.
     ISBN 0-06-039206-1
     1. Cookery, Italian.   2. Canning and preserving.
I. Title.
     TX723.D275     1997
     641.5945—dc21          97-654

97 98 99 00 01 ❖/RRD 10 9 8 7 6 5 4 3 2 1

*I am dedicating this book to
two of the best cooks I have ever known,
who taught me everything I know
to this day about providing a good meal
with the best ingredients:
my mother, Josephine,
and my mother-in-law, Arminda*

# CONTENTS

# ACKNOWLEDGMENTS

My first thanks go to Judith Regan, who had the imagination to encourage me in this project. Kristin Kiser was invaluable in her editorial guidance and support. My appreciation, too, for the work of my agent, Kay McCauley, and to Miriam Madden and Lauren Malis, who helped me tremendously in putting this book together.

# FOREWORD BY
# SENATOR ALFONSE D'AMATO

As the first Italian American United States senator from New York, I've had the privilege of eating at lots of great restaurants. But, without a doubt, my mamma's food is the best I've ever eaten. Bar none. I'd put Mamma up against the best chefs in New York, Rome, and Paris, and I know she'd win a blind taste test.

I'm not alone in that opinion. My dear friend, former New York City Mayor Ed Koch, simply loves Mamma's food. Whenever he comes to my parents' house in Long Island for Sunday dinner, he forgets his diet and can't stop eating. He raves about Mamma's cuisine for weeks.

Ed's not the only one. Another good friend, Howard Stern, can't get enough of my mamma's pasta. He's asked for her recipes. He goes on and on about her tomato sauce. He's told Mamma that she could put Paul Newman out of business.

The Senate is a busy place, with lots of fancy dinners. But the highlight of every year is the lunch that I host for about thirty senators, with my mother's food as the star attraction. It's incredible. For weeks, all I hear is, "When's Mamma coming?" Busy senators juggle important meetings to dine on my mamma's cooking. Although the Senate Dining Room is world-renowned for its bean soup, many of my colleagues would put Mamma's lasagna at the top of the menu.

This past year, Mamma came down to Washington to cook up a storm with my buddy Senator Ted Stevens of Alaska. You should have seen the two master chefs at work in Ted's small kitchen. And what a fantastic meal—with Mamma's pasta and Ted's fish. New Mexico's senior senator, Pete Domenici, and I must have gone back for fourths.

This has been going on for years. When I was growing up, all of the neighborhood kids wanted to stop by after school. Now, there were a lot of great cooks in Island Park in those days. But Mamma's food was legendary.

Make no mistake about it: Mamma's cooking has been a key ingredient in my success. In 1980, when I was running for my first term in the Senate, we printed up thousands of copies of a little cookbook, *Mamma D'Amato's Inflation-Fighting Recipes,* and couldn't hand them out fast enough. I won in a nail-biter, and I've always wondered if Mamma's recipes put me over the top.

I may be a United States senator, but I come from a line of great cooks. If I hadn't gone into politics, I might have opened a restaurant. My mother's father, Alfonso Cioffari, got his start in America by working in restaurants in New York City's Little Italy. After a successful career in the fur business, Grandpa Alfonso opened a restaurant named Brio near Rockefeller Center. All through the 1950s, Brio was a favorite of Hollywood stars, athletes, and even New York's mayor, Vincent Impellitteri. In the 1960s, Grandpa opened another successful restaurant, aptly named Alfonso's, across the street from the CBS studios. Ed Sullivan was a regular. My eldest son, Danny, is carrying on the family tradition. He's a keen student of Mamma's culinary techniques and regularly phones her for recipes. As readers will learn, the key to Mamma's cooking is her fresh ingredients, so Danny's become an expert canner of tomatoes. There aren't many Manhattan bachelors with dozens of cans of tomatoes in their apartments, but—I hear—Danny's dates don't mind his superb meals.

Mamma's food has long been the centerpiece of my family's life. It has kept our family close. Every Sunday Mamma puts on a big feast, with Christmas Eve and Easter the high points of the year. Although my schedule is tight, I try to make it home at least two Sundays a month. My brother Armand usually stops by, along with several of his five children. My daughters, Lorraine and Lisa, bring some of their seven children. My sons, Danny and Chris, try to drive out from Manhattan. It's quite a gathering of D'Amatos.

Before dinner, my father plays the piano. (When he was in college, his excellent piano-playing skills paid the bills.) Then we have some good Italian red wine and share in life's ups and downs. Mamma may start us off with some antipasto. Then she serves a pasta course, perhaps ravioli, and follows it with a spectacular veal or chicken dish. For a finale, there's always Mamma's freshly baked desserts.

I've brought many friends to my mamma's for Sunday dinner. My close friend, Ambassador Charles Gargano, is one of her favorites. I've often thought it's too bad that more people can't enjoy Mamma's homemade cuisine.

Over time, the word about Mamma's cooking has

spread. People are constantly asking me about Mamma's recipes. We've reprinted copies of the cookbook Mamma prepared for my 1980 campaign. People call her at home. Several years back, while I was writing my first book, I got the idea that Mamma should write a cookbook—that she owed it to people to share her recipes. Finally, after I wouldn't stop pestering her, Mamma relented. She agreed to share her culinary excellence with the world.

Mamma's food has brought much joy to the D'Amato family. I hope that her recipes and cooking techniques add much happiness to the life of your family as well. For remember, nothing matters more than family, and I know there's nothing like good food to keep a family together.

I love you, Mamma.

# INTRODUCTION

My mother used to tell us, "Before you're married, the way to a man's heart is through his stomach. After marriage, to keep his heart, you must feed him good food." My husband, Armand, has been eating my food for sixty years, and he tells everyone his good health is the true testimony of my cooking.

As far back as I can remember, our family has gathered around a table and shared food and companionship as a culinary adventure. My grandfather was an excellent cook. He had a large family and taught all of us to cook and bake, as well as to sew and press. Every Sunday we would learn something new, and we found all those skills useful later in our lives. My own father was even ahead of his time with some of the dishes he taught me to cook.

My father owned two diverse restaurants in New York City—the rich and famous flocked to Brio, and

This is my dad. Although he had retired from working in his restaurant, he always had to be doing *something*. At this time he was a cashier in a fish store in Floral Park, Long Island.

regular businesspeople and dockworkers gathered at Alfonso's. Since early childhood, I have spent an enormous amount of time in kitchens.

My own family of three children, eleven grandchildren, and seven great-grandchildren has always conferred, celebrated, and disagreed in the midst of my cooking. The kitchen is the heart of our family. I have fed politicians, celebrities, and people from all walks of life. And I've learned that a good offering of food along with some warmth of spirit always brings people together. I recently boarded a plane for Washington, D.C., to attend a party of politicians. I was armed with three pans of lasagna, and wouldn't you know, I was asked for a recipe then and there! Even important people have to eat.

My sister Vi's wedding to Jimmy Ciccimaro fifty-one years ago. I am standing next to the bride, and my husband, Armand—the best man—is seated third from left at the table. In the center of the table is a tray of those absolutely delicious Italian pastries and cookies—a must at an Italian wedding at that time.

It was my son, Senator Alfonse D'Amato, who thought I should put down in print what I've been serving up to generations of D'Amatos and our friends for almost my entire life.

Most of these recipes have been handed down within my family, and each member who adapted them has put his or her own signature on them or made an addition or change to a favorite.

My husband and I have worked side by side in our office most of our married life, and I know that when people come home from work they don't want to wait to eat or spend even more time in the kitchen preparing a meal.

The focus of this book maintains my cooking standards: buy and serve clean, fresh, fast, and economical food. I've tailored these recipes for busy working men and women.

# PASTA

Italians attribute success in business, sports, and love to eating pasta. I know you probably have some very popular and traditional recipes of your own. Here are some of my favorites; a few of them incorporate ideas that may be new to you.

Pasta is very easy to prepare, but there are some rules to follow. Always cook pasta in abundant boiling water, and in a pot large enough for it to move around. Add salt once the water is at a rolling boil, then toss in the pasta and stir. Stir it a few more times while it is cooking. The only way to know whether it is done or not is to taste it.

# Mamma D'Amato's Homemade Pasta Sauce I

3 cloves garlic, whole
3 tablespoons minced onion
2 tablespoons olive oil
4 pounds plum tomatoes, peeled, seeded, and chopped
Salt

In a medium saucepan, sauté garlic and onion in oil. When onion is translucent, discard garlic and add tomatoes. Season to taste with salt. Simmer for 45 minutes, until the sauce is thicker and has a little body.

*MAKES ABOUT 5 CUPS*

**MAMMA SAYS:** You can use canned tomatoes instead of fresh, but you need to add a little water to the mixture while it's cooking. Use a 28-ounce can of tomatoes per pound of pasta. But my tomato sauce (see pages 107–109) works the best.

# Mamma D'Amato's Homemade Pasta Sauce II

2 cloves garlic, whole
1 small onion, chopped
3 tablespoons olive oil
3 pounds plum tomatoes, peeled, seeded, and chopped
Salt

In a medium saucepan, sauté the garlic and onion in the olive oil for about 2 minutes, until the garlic is slightly golden. Add tomatoes and salt to taste. Simmer for 30 minutes, until the sauce has thickened.

*MAKES ABOUT 5 CUPS*

**MAMMA SAYS:** When you serve this over pasta, sprinkle on some chopped basil and pass around some grated cheese. You can also add some chopped prosciutto to the sauté for extra flavor.

My husband's family came over to dinner at our house back in 1962, and after a wonderful meal we pushed aside my dining room table and chairs, put on some records, and danced the night away.

# Spaghettini with Artichokes

Juice of 1 lemon
6 baby artichokes
4 tablespoons olive oil
2 cloves garlic, halved
1 teaspoon dried oregano
1 cup finely chopped mushrooms
Salt and pepper
3 tablespoons chicken or vegetable broth
¾ pound spaghettini
2 tablespoons butter
Grated Parmesan cheese

Add lemon juice to a bowl of cold water. Remove tough outer leaves from artichokes and trim off the tips. Cut each artichoke into eighths. Soak artichoke wedges in cold water with lemon juice for 1 hour.

Drain artichokes. In a large skillet, sauté artichokes briefly in olive oil. Cover and cook over medium heat for 5 minutes, until the artichokes soften and get a little darker.

Add garlic, oregano, and mushrooms. Season to taste with salt and pepper. Add 1 tablespoon broth and simmer about 10 minutes, adding broth 1 tablespoon at a time as needed until artichokes are tender. (If necessary, add water when all of the broth has been used.)

Meanwhile, in a large pot, cook spaghettini in abundant salted water until al dente.

Drain pasta and toss with butter and artichokes. Serve with grated Parmesan cheese on the side.

*SERVES 4*

# Pasta Puttanesca

2 ounces pancetta, finely chopped
3 tablespoons olive oil
8 cloves garlic, minced
1 (35-ounce) can peeled Italian tomatoes, with juice
3 anchovies, mashed
1 tablespoon capers
10 Kalamata olives, pitted and chopped
⅛ teaspoon crushed red pepper
2 tablespoons finely chopped fresh basil
1 pound pasta
3 tablespoons chopped fresh parsley
Grated Romano cheese
Pepper

Sauté pancetta in olive oil until crisp. Add garlic, sauté 30 seconds. Do not allow garlic to turn color.

Add tomatoes, anchovies, capers, olives, crushed pepper, and half of basil and stir. Simmer, uncovered, until sauce is thick, about 15 minutes. When sauce is almost ready, stir in remaining basil.

Meanwhile, in a large pot, cook pasta in abundant salted water and drain well.

In a large bowl, toss pasta with enough sauce to coat it. Sprinkle on parsley and remaining fresh basil.

Serve any extra sauce on the side, along with the grated cheese and pepper.

*SERVES 4 TO 6*

⊰ **MAMMA SAYS:** This is a spicy, tasty dish, just as the name—which means "of the prostitutes"—implies.

# Pasta with Broccoli

1 head broccoli
3 cloves garlic, whole
5 tablespoons olive oil
Crushed red pepper (optional)
Salt and pepper
1 pound ziti

Cut broccoli florets and tender stalks into small pieces; discard any tough stalks.

In a large pot, bring 3 quarts of water to a boil and cook broccoli about 5 minutes.

Meanwhile, in a skillet, fry the garlic cloves in oil (with red pepper if using). Crush the garlic after it softens and cook it until it browns. Remove the garlic with a slotted spoon and discard.

Remove broccoli from water with a slotted spoon and add to skillet, reserving broccoli cooking water. Season broccoli to taste with salt and pepper. Cover and cook until almost tender, about 10 minutes.

Return the broccoli cooking water to a boil, season with salt, and cook the ziti until al dente. When pasta is cooked, drain it and add it to the skillet. Cook 3 additional minutes over medium heat, stirring constantly.

*SERVES 4 TO 6*

# Fast Pasta Dish

1 clove garlic, minced
¼ pound pancetta or prosciutto, diced
2 tablespoons olive oil
6 plum tomatoes, peeled, seeded, and chopped
1 pound ziti
½ cup grated Parmesan cheese
2 tablespoons chopped fresh basil

In a large skillet, sauté garlic and pancetta or prosciutto in oil. When garlic is soft, after about 2 minutes, add tomatoes.

Meanwhile, in a large pot, cook ziti in abundant salted water until al dente. Drain and place in frying pan with tomatoes. Stir constantly while adding cheese.

Sprinkle on chopped basil when serving.

*SERVES 4 TO 6*

⊕ **MAMMA SAYS:** This is a fast pasta dish for busy working men and women. It is absolutely delicious!

# Grandsons' Pasta

3 eggs
3 tablespoons grated Romano cheese
2 tablespoons chopped fresh parsley
1 pound medium shells
8 tablespoons (1 stick) butter or margarine
Pepper

Beat eggs with grated cheese and parsley and set aside.

Cook shells in a large pot of abundant salted water until al dente. Remove pasta to a colander with a slotted spoon. Reserve ½ cup pasta cooking water.

Return pasta and reserved water to pot and add butter. Cook over medium heat, stirring constantly, until butter is melted. Add egg mixture and continue stirring constantly until eggs are cooked through. Season to taste with pepper.

*SERVES 4 TO 6*

⌐ **MAMMA SAYS:** This is a dish that my grandsons love and request continually.

# Quick Linguine with Clams and Shrimp

1 tablespoon olive oil
1 tablespoon chopped onion
1 clove garlic, minced
1 (7-ounce) can chopped clams, with juice
1 (7-ounce) can shrimp, drained and rinsed
1 (8-ounce) bottle clam juice
1 pound linguine
2 tablespoons chopped fresh parsley
Pepper

Heat oil in a skillet and sauté onion and garlic for about 2 minutes, until soft. Add shrimp and cook 3 minutes, until pink. Add chopped clams and clam juice and simmer 10 minutes.

Meanwhile, in a large pot, cook linguine until al dente. Drain and place in serving bowl. Toss with clam sauce and sprinkle with parsley. Season to taste with pepper.

*SERVES 4*

My husband, Armand, and Al's son Christopher watch me feed Al some of my famous lasagna—he's always got his mouth open, giving speeches or eating my food!

# Lasagna

1 pound ricotta cheese
1 egg
¼ cup chopped fresh parsley
¼ cup grated Romano cheese
Salt and pepper
1 pound Italian sausage
1 pound ground beef
1 (8-ounce) package lasagna noodles
¼ pound mozzarella cheese, thinly sliced
2 quarts tomato sauce (see pages 107–109)

Preheat oven to 400 degrees.

Combine ricotta cheese, egg, parsley, and Romano cheese. Season to taste with salt and pepper.

Dice Italian sausage and brown along with ground beef.

In a large pot, cook lasagna noodles in abundant salted water until they are al dente.

Cover the bottom of a 9½ × 13½-inch pan with lasagna noodles. Cover with a layer of mozzarella, ricotta mixture, and add some sauce on top. Top sauce with some of the beef and sausage combination, then top the meat with more noodles.

Continue adding layers in this order until pan is full, ending with sauce. Bake for 30 minutes. Take pan out and cover with aluminum foil. Turn oven down to 300 degrees and bake for another 30 minutes.

Allow to set for a few minutes before serving.

*SERVES 8 TO 10*

# Pasta with Beans

1 cup dried white beans
3 cloves garlic
5 tablespoons olive oil
1 cup tomato sauce (see pages 107–109)
Salt and pepper
1 pound small shell pasta

Soak beans overnight in abundant cold water.

Drain beans, place in a 2-quart pot, and add water to cover. Bring beans to a boil, then turn down to a simmer. Chop 1 clove garlic and add to beans. Cover beans and cook until tender, about 1 hour and 30 minutes. (If beans appear to be drying out, add small amounts of hot water.)

Meanwhile, place oil in a small saucepan, add remaining garlic, and brown slowly, smashing the garlic as it cooks.

When garlic has browned, remove and discard it and add tomato sauce. Season to taste with salt and pepper and set aside.

When beans are cooked and have absorbed most of the water, stir in tomato sauce and simmer another 20 minutes, until of medium-thick consistency.

Meanwhile, in a large pot, cook pasta in abundant salted water. Drain, transfer to serving bowl, and top with sauce.

*SERVES 4 TO 6*

# Stuffed Shells

1 (10-ounce) box frozen chopped spinach
1 egg, beaten
1 pound ground beef
½ cup grated Parmesan cheese
8 ounces mozzarella cheese, chopped
Salt and pepper
1 pound large shells
2 cups tomato sauce (see pages 107–109)

Preheat oven to 350 degrees.

Cook spinach according to package instructions. Run under cold water, then squeeze out as much moisture as possible.

Mix spinach with egg, beef, and cheeses. Season to taste with salt and pepper.

Meanwhile, in a large pot, cook shells in abundant salted water until al dente. Drain in a colander and run under cold water until cool enough to handle.

Spread 1 cup tomato sauce on the bottom of a 9½ × 13½-inch pan.

Stuff each shell with beef and spinach mixture. Place shells in pan in a single layer. Top with remaining tomato sauce.

Bake for 45 minutes.

*SERVES 4 TO 6*

◁ **MAMMA SAYS:** You can also replace the beef and spinach in the filling with ricotta.

# RICE

Rice dishes are Italian classics, like the famous Italian dish called risotto.

Any rice dish is simple to prepare, nutritious, and economical. Italian rice holds the flavor of the ingredients to an unusual extent, and it remains firm.

# Baked Rice with Peas and Mushrooms

6 tablespoons butter
1 cup long-grain white rice, uncooked
4 cups chicken broth
1 small green bell pepper, seeded and chopped
1 clove garlic, minced
½ pound mushrooms, sliced
1 cup cooked peas
¼ cup grated Parmesan cheese
Salt and pepper

Preheat oven to 350 degrees.

Melt butter in a small heavy skillet and brown rice evenly. In a large baking dish, combine browned rice, chicken broth, green pepper, garlic, mushrooms, peas, and cheese. Season to taste with salt and pepper, stir, and cover dish tightly with aluminum foil.

Bake for 30 minutes.

*SERVES 4 TO 6*

# Liver with Rice

1½ pounds calf's liver
1 small onion, chopped
2 tablespoons olive oil
½ teaspoon dried oregano
Salt
¼ cup red wine vinegar
3 cups cooked rice

Cut liver into cubes. In a large skillet, fry liver and onion in oil over medium heat, stirring constantly, until the liver is no longer red, about 5 minutes.

Sprinkle on oregano and season to taste with salt. Add ¼ cup water, cover, and simmer 5 minutes. Uncover and stir in vinegar.

Serve over rice.

*SERVES 4 TO 6*

# Vegetables and Rice with Chicken Cutlets

4 medium-size chicken cutlets
1 egg, beaten
½ cup Italian bread crumbs
½ cup olive oil
½ pound mushrooms, quartered
1 small onion, thinly sliced
1 small green bell pepper, seeded and thinly sliced
1 large tomato, seeded and diced
4 scallions, sliced
1 cup uncooked rice
2 tablespoons soy sauce
¼ cup good dry white wine

Preheat oven to 350 degrees.

Dip cutlets in egg and then dredge in Italian bread crumbs. Pan-fry on both sides in ¼ cup olive oil until lightly browned.

In a separate pan, sauté mushrooms, onion, green pepper, tomato, and scallions in remaining ¼ cup oil.

Boil rice with 2 cups of water according to package directions.

In a large bowl combine cooked rice and vegetables. Cut chicken cutlets into cubes and stir into rice along with soy sauce and wine.

Place in baking dish and bake 20 minutes, until just heated through.

*SERVES 4 TO 6*

# Seafood Risotto

6 littleneck clams in the shell
12 mussels in the shell
2 tablespoons butter
2 tablespoons olive oil
2 tablespoons chopped celery
2 tablespoons chopped onion
2 cloves garlic, minced
1 cup long-grain rice, uncooked
Salt and pepper
2 cups chicken broth
¼ cup grated Provolone cheese
¼ cup chopped fresh parsley

Thoroughly clean clams and mussels. Place clams and mussels in a large skillet with 1 inch water. Cover and steam about 5 minutes, until shells have opened. (Discard any unopened shellfish.)

Remove clams and mussels with a slotted spoon, reserving liquid. Remove clam and mussel meat from shells and set aside.

Place butter and oil in a large, heavy skillet. Melt butter over medium heat. Add celery, onion, garlic, and rice. Brown over high heat. Season to taste with salt and pepper.

Add about ¼ cup chicken broth. Stir until broth is absorbed. Continue to add broth, about ¼ cup at a time, stirring constantly and allowing rice to absorb broth between each addition, until rice is cooked through, about 20 minutes.

Add Provolone cheese and stir in mussels and clams with some of the reserved steaming water. Sprinkle on parsley.

*SERVES 4 TO 6*

⊰ **MAMMA SAYS:** You can add cooked shrimp to this recipe if you wish. Stir in with mussels and clams.

# Risotto Milanese

8 tablespoons (1 stick) butter or margarine
1½ cups rice
1 quart chicken broth
1 pinch saffron
½ cup grated Parmesan cheese

Melt butter in a large stockpot. Add rice to stockpot and stir until coated with butter.

Add ¼ cup chicken broth and stir. Then add saffron and stir until broth is absorbed. Continue to add broth, about ¼ cup at a time, stirring constantly and allowing rice to absorb broth between each addition, until rice is cooked through, about 20 minutes.

Serve with grated cheese.

*SERVES 4 TO 6*

◁ **MAMMA SAYS:** I prefer to use Uncle Ben's rice in this recipe.

# SOUP

Every mother, no matter what her ethnic background may be, is convinced that good health and love emanate from soup. My soups are just about as popular with my family as my jarred tomato sauce. I often prepare soups for "transport" to family and friends for easing colds and flu, as well as for welcome-home-from-the-hospital consumption.

Here are a few hearty and healthy ones from my kitchen.

# Escarole and Bean Soup

1 head escarole
4 cups chicken broth
8 cloves garlic, minced
2 cups cooked white beans, preferably navy beans
Salt and pepper
¼ cup olive oil

Clean escarole and remove any tough stems. Chop roughly.

In a large heavy pot, combine chicken broth, escarole, and garlic. Bring to a boil, lower heat, and simmer for ½ hour. Stir in beans and season to taste with salt and pepper. Remove from heat and drizzle olive oil on top.

*SERVES 4 TO 6*

☙ **MAMMA SAYS:** To prepare beans, soak them overnight in abundant cold water. In the morning, drain and rinse the beans and place them in a pot with abundant water. Bring to a boil, then simmer, uncovered, until tender, approximately 1 hour and 30 minutes. You can also use canned beans, but remember to rinse them first.

# Instant Meatball Soup

2 large carrots, peeled and diced
3 large celery stalks, diced
1 onion, diced
4 chicken bouillon cubes
½ pound ground beef
Salt and pepper
l egg, lightly beaten
½ cup grated Parmesan or Romano cheese

In a large saucepan or soup kettle, bring 4 quarts water to a boil. Add carrots, celery, and onion. Cover and cook until vegetables are tender, about ½ hour. Add bouillon cubes and lower heat to a simmer.

Season ground beef with salt and pepper. Mix beef with egg and half of grated cheese. Shape beef into tiny meatballs (½-inch in diameter).

Add meatballs to soup and simmer briskly until meat is cooked through, about 3 to 5 minutes.

Serve with remaining grated cheese.

*SERVES 6*

❧ **MAMMA SAYS:** Cooked pasta or rice may be added before serving.

# Lentil Soup

1 cup lentils
4 slices bacon, diced
1 clove garlic
3 tablespoons tomato sauce (see pages 107–109)
1 tablespoon chopped fresh parsley
Salt and pepper

Rinse lentils and set aside to drain.

Sauté bacon in large saucepan with garlic clove until garlic is golden brown. Discard garlic. Stir in tomato sauce. Add 2 cups water and bring to a rolling boil. Add lentils.

Simmer over medium heat until lentils are tender, about 30 to 45 minutes, adding more water if lentils look dry. Stir in parsley. Season to taste with salt and pepper.

*SERVES 4*

∢ **MAMMA SAYS:** Cooked small macaroni may be added to soup before serving.

# Beef Soup

3 large carrots, peeled
4 large celery stalks
1 onion
2 pounds beef hind shank with bone
½ cup tomato sauce (see page 107)
Salt

Grind carrots, celery stalks, and onion in a food processor or blender.

Place meat in a large stockpot with 4 cups water and bring to a boil. Skim off any foam. Add tomato sauce and return broth to a boil. Skim off any additional foam, then add the ground vegetables. Season with salt to taste.

Turn down to a low boil, cover the pot (leaving a crack for steam to escape), and continue cooking until meat is tender, about an hour.

*SERVES 4 TO 6*

꿍 **MAMMA SAYS:** You may add cooked pastina to this soup.

# Potato Soup

3 small potatoes, peeled and diced
Salt
1 quart milk
2 slices onion
3 tablespoons butter
1 tablespoon flour
¼ teaspoon celery salt
1 pinch cayenne pepper
1 teaspoon chopped fresh parsley

In a large saucepot, cook potatoes, covered, in boiling salted water for about 10 minutes, until soft. Drain in a colander, then return to empty pot.

Place milk in a small saucepan with onion and bring to a boil. Remove onion and discard. Slowly add hot milk to potatoes over medium heat, beating with a whisk.

Melt half the butter and add it to the potatoes. Stir in flour, celery salt, and cayenne pepper. Season to taste with salt. Boil 1 minute, strain into serving bowl, stir in remaining butter until melted. Sprinkle with parsley.

*SERVES 4 TO 6*

❧ **MAMMA SAYS:** This is a pretty thick version of potato soup. If you prefer a lighter soup, thin it with additional hot milk.

# CHICKEN

Years ago, we would go to the chicken farm and get fresh birds and bring them home. We salted them and put them aside. Chicken is delicious when salted with regular and garlic salt and then stored in the fridge (for no longer than 2 days) or freezer (indefinitely) to use later. I do this in fairly large quantities because I never know who is coming to dinner!

My grandson Dan brought his friends over recently, and I had chicken on hand. While they were eating, Dan's brother, Chris, called from the airport on his return from London. "I'm starved, Mamma," he said. "Save whatever is left over from Dan and his friends for me." Needless to say, nothing was left after Dan and his friends had finished. That was one time I wished I had put aside more chicken.

# Breaded Chicken

¼ cup bread crumbs
½ cup grated Parmesan cheese
2 tablespoons butter
2 whole boneless chicken breasts, totaling about 1½
    pounds
Salt and pepper

Preheat oven to 375 degrees.
Combine bread crumbs and cheese.
Butter a large baking dish and set aside.
Halve chicken breasts and roll in bread crumb mixture.
Place in buttered baking dish.
Put a pat of butter on top of each chicken breast and
season to taste with salt and pepper.
Bake for 1 hour and 45 minutes.

*SERVES 4 TO 6*

**MAMMA SAYS:** This recipe makes a good company dish
and takes little effort. It can be prepared in advance and
stored in the fridge. Reheat in a 325-degree oven for 30
minutes.

# Chicken Cacciatore

1 (3-pound) chicken, cut into eighths
2 tablespoons olive oil, or any other oil
1 clove garlic, minced
½ teaspoon dried oregano
½ cup tomato sauce (see pages 107–109)
1 teaspoon capers
Salt and pepper
¼ cup loosely packed fresh basil leaves

In a large heavy skillet, brown chicken pieces on both sides in oil over medium-high heat. (You may need to do this in batches if skillet is not large enough.) Add minced garlic, oregano, tomato sauce, and capers. Season to taste with salt and pepper. Cover and cook over medium heat until chicken is tender, about 15 minutes.

Uncover and add basil.

*SERVES 4 TO 6*

Al's two sons, Christopher (left) and Danny (right), sitting on their Grandpa Armand's lap.

# Chicken Scallopini

6 chicken cutlets, totaling about 1 pound
¼ cup flour
3 tablespoons butter
½ cup vegetable oil
1 clove garlic, minced
¼ teaspoon dried rosemary
¼ teaspoon dried oregano
¼ cup lemon juice
Salt and pepper
1 (4-ounce) can sliced mushrooms, drained
¼ cup chopped fresh parsley

Lightly dredge cutlets in flour.

Heat butter and oil in a large heavy skillet over medium heat. When hot, add chicken cutlets and brown. (You may need to do this in batches if skillet is not large enough.) When cutlets are browned on both sides, add minced garlic, rosemary, oregano, and lemon juice. Season to taste with salt and pepper. Cover immediately and simmer 2 to 3 minutes. Add mushrooms. Cover again and cook for about 5 minutes.

Sprinkle on chopped parsley.

*SERVES 4 TO 6*

**MAMMA SAYS:** A nice young fellow once asked me why I use lemon juice in my Chicken Scallopini instead of the traditional wine. "Well," I explained, "one must use *good* wine to cook and that's not always available, and besides, you only need a little wine and then you've got the whole bottle. So lemon is great. It adds more zest and is less expensive. I think there is more flavor with lemon too. Do you cook?" I asked him. "Yes," he said. "Do you have a girlfriend you are going to cook for?" "Yes," he said. So I said, "Well, enjoy the wine with her at dinner and save the money for celebrating." He liked that idea.

# Balsamic Chicken

¼ cup flour
Salt and pepper
4 boneless, skinless chicken breasts, halved, totaling
    about 2 pounds
4 tablespoons olive or vegetable oil
1 clove garlic, minced
1 teaspoon oregano
6 tablespoons balsamic vinegar

Season flour with salt and pepper and dredge chicken breasts in seasoned flour.

Heat oil in a large heavy skillet. Place chicken breasts in skillet and brown on both sides over medium heat.

Add minced garlic, oregano, and vinegar, then cover and cook over low heat until chicken is tender, about 15 minutes.

*SERVES 4 TO 6*

**MAMMA SAYS:** This dish has a piquant taste similar to that of chicken cooked in wine.

# Chicken with Peppers and Onions

2 chicken breasts, halved, totaling about 1 pound
4 tablespoons olive oil
6 long light green Italian frying peppers, diced
1 large onion, sliced
½ cup tomato sauce (see pages 107–109)
Salt

In a large heavy skillet, brown chicken breasts in oil over medium heat.

Add peppers, onion, and tomato sauce to chicken. Cook over medium heat for about 15 minutes, stirring occasionally, until peppers and onion are soft and the chicken is tender.

Season to taste with salt.

*SERVES 3 TO 4*

# MEAT

There is a lot of controversy about meat today. My motto is, just about anything in moderation. I think that meat dishes still have a place on the American menu. They are particularly good when the weather turns cold, or after a tiring workday, or when one is convalescing.

The cuts do not have to be expensive, and portions do not have to be hefty. Nothing smells better when you walk into a home on a weekend than the aroma of a meat dish or a roast wafting through the house. The smell brings back memories of Sundays and holidays with my family.

# Brisket of Beef

2 tablespoons vegetable oil
1 clove garlic, minced
1 large onion, sliced
1 (4-pound) brisket of beef
3 carrots, peeled and roughly chopped
4 large potatoes, peeled and roughly chopped
1 cup tomato sauce (see pages 107–109)
1 (8-ounce) can beef gravy
4 tablespoons balsamic vinegar
2 tablespoons Worcestershire sauce
Salt and pepper

Preheat oven to 325 degrees.

Heat oil in a large heavy skillet over medium heat and fry garlic and onion until onion is transparent, about 3 to 4 minutes.

Remove garlic and onion and reserve. Place meat in same skillet over high heat and brown 10 minutes on each side. Remove from skillet.

Spread carrots, potatoes, and onion and garlic in a roasting pan. Place meat on top.

Whisk together tomato sauce, beef gravy, balsamic vinegar, and Worcestershire sauce and pour over meat and vegetables. Season to taste with salt and pepper.

Roast, covered, for 3 hours. Test for doneness by inserting a fork in the meat; it should penetrate easily.

*SERVES 4 TO 6*

⊛ **MAMMA SAYS:** You can also place all ingredients in a crockpot and cook on low for about 10 hours. If you start it before going to work, it will be ready at dinnertime.

# Chow Mein à la Mamma D'Amato

1 pound shrimp, peeled and deveined
4 tablespoons butter
¼ cup vegetable oil
½ pound lean pork, diced
5 large stalks celery with leaves, chopped
2 large onions, thinly sliced
1 can Chinese vegetables, drained
¼ cup soy sauce

Cut shrimp in half. In a large skillet, sauté shrimp in butter and oil over medium heat. After about 3 minutes, when shrimp are pink, remove with a slotted spoon and set aside.

Sauté pork over medium heat for about 3 minutes in the same skillet. When cooked through, remove with a slotted spoon and set aside.

In the same skillet, sauté celery and onions over medium heat for about 30 minutes, until soft. Add Chinese vegetables and soy sauce.

When vegetables are heated through, add the shrimp and pork and cook over medium heat, stirring constantly, until all ingredients are hot.

*SERVES 3 TO 4*

❧ **MAMMA SAYS:** Serve this over rice or noodles. If desired, add a cube of chicken bouillon to water when making rice.

# Stew

4 tablespoons vegetable oil
½ pound beef, cut into chunks
½ pound veal, cut into chunks
½ pound lamb, cut into chunks
1 onion, thinly sliced
½ cup tomato sauce (see pages 107–109)
2 carrots, peeled and chopped
2 potatoes, peeled and chopped
1 (10-ounce) package frozen peas
1 bay leaf
Salt and pepper

Heat oil in a large dutch oven and brown beef, veal, and lamb over medium heat for about 15 to 20 minutes. Add thinly sliced onion and sauté over medium heat until soft, about 5 minutes. Add tomato sauce and simmer for 10 minutes. Add carrots, potatoes, peas, and bay leaf.

Season to taste with salt and pepper, cover tightly, and cook over low heat until vegetables are soft, about 20 minutes.

Remove bay leaf before serving.

*SERVES 4 TO 6*

# Veal Steak

1½ pounds veal shoulder steak with bone
3 tablespoons butter
3 tablespoons oil
1½ cups uncooked rice
1 quart chicken broth

Preheat oven to 325 degrees.

In a large skillet, sauté veal in butter and oil over medium heat until it browns, about 5 minutes.

Place rice and chicken broth in a large baking dish. Stir to combine, then place meat on top.

Cover and bake until rice is cooked and liquid absorbed, about 30 minutes.

*SERVES 4 TO 6*

Dinner, as usual, at my house (1975). Penny D'Amato is on the left and Al and Penny's daughter Lisa is on the right.

# Veal Rollatini

1 ounce mozzarella cheese
6 veal cutlets, flattened, totaling about 1 pound
6 slices prosciutto
2 tablespoons grated Parmesan or Romano cheese
¼ cup chopped fresh parsley
2 tablespoons butter
2 tablespoons oil
1 clove garlic, minced
½ teaspoon rosemary
Salt
½ cup lemon juice
12 ounces mushrooms, sliced

Cut mozzarella into six thin pieces.

Place a cutlet on a flat surface. Place a slice of prosciutto and a piece of mozzarella on top of one of the cutlets. Sprinkle on one-sixth of the grated cheese and one-sixth of the parsley. Roll cutlet up and secure with a toothpick. Repeat with remaining cutlets.

Place butter and oil in a large frying pan. Melt butter, then brown the rollatini on all sides over medium heat for about 3 to 4 minutes.

Add garlic and rosemary and sauté for about 3 minutes over medium heat. Season to taste with salt, add lemon juice, and cover. Cook 3 minutes over medium heat, then add sliced mushrooms, cover again, and cook for 10 additional minutes, stirring occasionally.

*SERVES 4 TO 6*

✀ **MAMMA SAYS:** You can make this with chicken cutlets in place of the veal if you like. Either way, don't forget to remove the toothpicks before serving!

# Veal and Mushroom Oreganata

3 large portobello mushroom caps
2 tablespoons plus 1 teaspoon olive oil
Salt and pepper
6 veal cutlets, totaling about 1 pound
½ cup lemon juice
½ cup chicken broth
1 teaspoon oregano

Preheat oven to 425 degrees. Brush mushrooms with 1 tablespoon oil and season to taste with salt and pepper. Roast mushrooms on a cookie sheet for 12 minutes, until they are dark brown in color. Slice cooked mushrooms and set aside.

Rub cutlets with 1 tablespoon oil. Season to taste with salt and pepper. In a large heavy skillet, brown cutlets about 8 minutes on each side in remaining oil over medium heat.

Remove cutlets to platter and skim off fat. Add lemon juice, chicken broth, and oregano to skillet and reduce by half. Stir in sliced mushrooms and cook another 2 minutes. Spoon over veal.

*SERVES 4 TO 6*

# Veal Kidneys

3 veal kidneys
3 tablespoons oil
1 small onion, sliced
Salt and pepper
½ cup red wine vinegar
1 teaspoon oregano

Discard any fat from kidneys and cut kidneys into chunks.

Place kidneys in a large skillet. Cover and steam over low heat for 5 minutes. Drain the water from the pan and then steam the kidneys again for another 5 minutes. Drain the liquid again.

Return kidneys to skillet along with oil and onion. Season to taste with salt and pepper and sauté over medium heat for 5 minutes, until onion is translucent. Add vinegar and oregano and cook for 5 minutes.

*SERVES 3 TO 4*

# Pepper Pork Chops

2 potatoes
4 tablespoons vegetable oil
6 medium pork chops
3 green bell peppers, seeded and sliced
3 vinegar (pickled) peppers
¼ cup vinegar from pepper jar
Salt and pepper

Peel and cube potatoes and parboil, in water to cover, for 5 minutes over medium heat.

Heat vegetable oil in a large heavy skillet and brown pork chops on both sides over medium heat, about 3 to 5 minutes per side.

Remove pork chops with a slotted spoon and add sliced bell peppers to pan. Cook peppers over medium heat for 5 minutes, until slightly tender.

Return pork chops to pan and add potatoes, vinegar peppers, and vinegar. Cover and cook over medium heat for 5 to 10 minutes. Season with salt and pepper to taste.

*SERVES 4*

**MAMMA SAYS:** This dish is delicious. The vinegar—an old Neapolitan trick—gives it great flavor. You can do chicken this way too. And always keep in mind, the better the cut of chicken, fish, or meat, the tastier the dish will be.

# Roasted Lamb Shanks

4 lamb shanks, totaling about 2 pounds
2 cloves garlic, thinly sliced
2 tablespoons soy sauce
Salt and pepper
1 small onion, sliced
½ cup lemon juice

Preheat oven to 350 degrees.

Make slits in lamb shanks and insert garlic slices.

Rub shanks with soy sauce and season to taste with salt and pepper. Put onion slices in bottom of roasting pan and place lamb shanks on top. Pour lemon juice over shanks.

Roast for 45 minutes. The lamb should be brown and tender.

*SERVES 4*

# Roast Leg of Lamb

1 (6- to 7-pound) leg of lamb, boned and butterflied
2 sprigs parsley, chopped
3 cloves garlic, whole
Salt and pepper
2 tablespoons vegetable oil
¼ cup balsamic vinegar

Preheat oven to 400 degrees.

Lay lamb flat and stuff with parsley and 2 cloves garlic. Season to taste with salt and pepper.

Roll up lamb and tie securely. Brush with oil. Slice remaining garlic clove. Make some cuts in the meat and put garlic slices into the cuts.

Roast in a large baking pan, sprinkling the lamb with vinegar every 10 minutes as you turn it.

After about 45 minutes, when lamb is golden on all sides, lower heat to 300 degrees and roast for 1 additional hour. The meat should be pink inside.

*SERVES 6*

# Meatloaf

1 pound ground beef
1 small clove garlic, minced
½ envelope Lipton Onion Soup mix
3 tablespoons grated Parmesan or Romano cheese
4 tablespoons plain bread crumbs
1 egg, lightly beaten
2 hard-boiled eggs
2 tablespoons olive oil

Preheat oven to 375 degrees.

Combine ground beef, garlic, soup mix, grated cheese, 2 tablespoons bread crumbs, beaten egg, and ¾ cup water. Mix well with your hands.

Sprinkle remaining bread crumbs on a large piece of aluminum foil. Spread meat mixture on top of bread crumbs. Slice hard-boiled eggs in half and arrange on meat. Roll meat jelly-roll fashion in aluminum foil, keeping it covered with bread crumbs.

Brush a baking pan with 1 tablespoon oil. Unwrap meatloaf onto pan and drizzle remaining oil over it. Bake for 1 hour. It should be firm to the touch.

*SERVES 4 TO 6*

# Italian Meatballs

1 pound ground beef
1 pound ground pork
1 clove garlic, minced
1 sprig parsley, chopped
2 eggs, beaten
¼ cup bread crumbs
¼ cup grated Parmesan or Romano cheese
Salt and pepper

Preheat oven to 350 degrees.

Combine all ingredients. Mix with your hands and form into balls 1½ inches in diameter. Place on rack in roasting pan and bake for 40 minutes, turning once. The meatballs should be firm to the touch. Serve with tomato sauce and pasta.

*SERVES 4 TO 6*

~ **MAMMA SAYS:** For crunchier meatballs, fry these in about 3 tablespoons of oil rather than baking them. Brown on both sides over medium heat, 5 minutes per side.

# Liver and Bacon

3 slices calf's liver
6 strips bacon

Preheat broiler.

Wrap two strips of bacon around each slice of liver, covering both sides completely. Press to adhere bacon to liver.

Broil, turning once, until bacon is crisp and liver is brown.

*SERVES 3*

❧ **MAMMA SAYS:** Serve this with lemon wedges.

# Braciola

1 pound shoulder steak, unsliced
1 slice prosciutto
2 cloves garlic, minced
⅛ cup grated Parmesan or Romano cheese
1 sprig parsley, chopped
2 ounces mozzarella cheese, diced
Salt and pepper
4 tablespoons olive oil
½ cup tomato sauce (see pages 107–109)
¼ cup chopped onion

Pound steak to a thickness of about ¼ inch.

Place prosciutto slice on steak and sprinkle on half of garlic, grated cheese, parsley, and mozzarella. Season to taste with salt and pepper. Roll steak up to form a cylinder and secure by tying with string or inserting toothpicks at 1 ½-inch intervals.

Heat oil in a large skillet and brown meat on all sides over medium heat.

Mix tomato sauce, onion, and remaining garlic and pour over meat.

Cover and simmer about 30 minutes.

*SERVES 3 TO 4*

⌁ **MAMMA SAYS:** If you want to serve this with macaroni or any other kind of pasta, increase the tomato sauce to 2 cups.

# FISH

Fish is sometimes difficult to introduce, especially in families with younger members. My husband's mother never cooked it, but I have taught him to like it. It's an amusing story.

I made a very thick tuna steak one time for my husband and served it with veggies and rice. I set the table and put the dish down at his place. Just as he went to sit down, he exchanged his regular knife for a steak knife. I didn't say a word. He took a bite and said, "This is a delicious piece of meat. What kind is it?" I laughed and told him it was fish.

Another time one of my grandsons called and said, "Mamma, I want to make some fish, but I just don't know how." He likes to cook, but he needs his dishes to be fast because he comes home late and is very hungry by the time he gets there. I told him to get a nice thick slice of fish and then make a paste of bread crumbs seasoned with garlic, parsley, cheese, and a little oil and pat it on top of the fish. Place the fish in a pan that can cook on top of the stove as well as under the broiler. Put it on the stove and let it cook for about 3 minutes on one side, and then put it under the broiler and broil until golden brown, at least 5 to 8 minutes. This is the best way to cook a thick piece of fish so that you are sure it will be cooked through, and it's very easy. My grandson liked it, and I'm sure you will too.

# Balsamic Tuna Steak

1 tuna steak, about 1 pound
¼ cup flour
4 tablespoons olive oil
1 clove garlic, minced
1 small onion, chopped
2 tablespoons balsamic vinegar
Salt and pepper

Dredge tuna in flour.

Heat oil in a heavy skillet over high heat and quickly brown tuna on both sides. Remove tuna from heat and transfer to a clean skillet.

In the skillet in which the tuna was cooked, sauté garlic and onion for 5 minutes, until soft. Deglaze with balsamic vinegar and pour over tuna steak.

Season tuna to taste with salt and pepper. Cook over medium heat for 5 minutes. Test for doneness using a fork.

*SERVES 2*

**MAMMA SAYS:** Although my husband didn't eat fish when we met, this dish is now one of his favorites.

# Broiled Scrod

1 cup bread crumbs
¼ cup chopped fresh parsley
2 tablespoons grated Parmesan cheese
1 clove garlic, minced
2 tablespoons olive oil
1 thick piece scrod, about 1 pound
Lemon wedges

Preheat broiler.

Combine bread crumbs, chopped parsley, grated cheese, garlic, and oil. Mix thoroughly.

Pat mixture on both sides of fish and place in an oven-proof skillet.

Cook scrod over medium heat for 2 minutes and then place under broiler until golden brown.

Serve with lemon wedges.

*SERVES 2*

Dinner at my mother's apartment. My father and my husband are with me and Mom.

# Baccalà Salad

1 thick 1-pound piece baccalà (see "Mamma Says,"
   below)
4 tablespoons olive oil
2 cloves garlic, minced
¼ cup chopped fresh parsley
Juice of 1 lemon
2 vinegar (pickled) peppers, diced
¼ cup black or green olives, pitted and chopped

Soak baccalà in water until soft, about 2 days or more
according to thickness, changing water daily.

In a saucepan, boil baccalà in water to cover for 20
minutes. Drain and chop.

Toss baccalà with olive oil, garlic, parsley, lemon juice,
vinegar peppers, and olives. Serve cold.

*SERVES 4 TO 6*

**MAMMA SAYS:** Baccalà is salted, dried codfish. You can
   find it in Italian specialty stores. It can sometimes be
   purchased already soaked and softened, and in that case
   you can skip the soaking step in the recipe. This recipe is
   a traditional family favorite for Christmas Eve.

# VEGETABLES

You don't need one more person to tell you how healthy it is for you to eat vegetables. Our mothers have been telling us this for years—and now nutritionists and diet counselors are suggesting vegetable dishes as main courses for a perfectly balanced diet. This proves you should always listen to your mother, because mothers know what's best for you.

A number of these recipes can be used as appetizers or luncheon entrées.

# Spinach and Sausage Pie

**CRUST**
1 cup flour
½ teaspoon salt
⅓ cup plus 1 tablespoon Crisco

**FILLING**
1 pound Italian sausage
1 tablespoon olive oil
2 (10-ounce) packages frozen spinach
6 eggs
½ pound shredded mozzarella cheese
1 pound ricotta cheese
⅛ teaspoon garlic powder
Salt and pepper

Preheat oven to 375 degrees.

To make the crust, place flour and salt in a bowl. Use a pastry blender or fork to cut in Crisco. Stir in ⅓ cup water and knead to incorporate.

Roll out dough, place in a 9-inch pie plate, and trim off excess. Set aside.

To make filling, cook sausage in olive oil over medium heat until browned. Set aside.

Cook spinach according to package instructions. Run under cold water and then squeeze out as much moisture as possible.

In a large bowl, beat eggs. Add mozzarella and ricotta and beat well to combine. Then add cooked sausage and spinach and garlic powder. Season to taste with salt and pepper.

Pour filling into crust. Bake until crust browns, 1 hour and 15 minutes.

*SERVES 6*

᭝ **MAMMA SAYS:** With a salad, some bread, and a glass of wine, this makes a nice, light lunch.

# Sausage, Peppers, and Potatoes

6 potatoes
1 onion, sliced
3 green or red bell peppers, seeded and sliced
2 cloves garlic, minced
Salt and pepper
1½ pounds Italian sausage

Preheat oven to 400 degrees.

Peel potatoes and cut into wedges.

Layer potatoes, onion slices, and peppers in a baking dish and sprinkle with garlic. Season to taste with salt and pepper.

Lay sausages on top of mixture and prick each sausage with a fork several times.

Bake until mixture browns, 1 hour and 30 minutes.

*SERVES 4 TO 6*

⌐ **MAMMA SAYS:** This dish is a bit different, but don't be put off. It is so tasty.

# Sausage with Savoy Cabbage

1 head Savoy cabbage
¼ cup olive oil or vegetable oil
6 links pork sausage with fennel seed
2 cloves garlic, minced
Salt and pepper

Rinse cabbage and drain. Cut into segments, blanch by plunging in a pot of boiling water and removing after a minute, and set aside.

Heat half the oil in a skillet over medium flame and add sausage. Cook, turning as necessary, until golden brown and cooked through, about 10 minutes. Remove from pan and set aside.

Heat remaining oil in a casserole over medium flame and add cabbage and garlic. Season to taste with salt and pepper. Cover tightly and simmer about 15 minutes, until cabbage softens. If it is sticking, add just enough boiling water to moisten it. Stir occasionally.

Add sausage to cabbage, cover, and cook over medium heat until sausage browns, another 15 minutes.

*SERVES 4 TO 6*

◈ **MAMMA SAYS:** This is a great dish on a cold night. With some bread and salad, it becomes a meal.

# Frittata with Leftovers

3 eggs
2 tablespoons grated Parmesan cheese
1 tablespoon chopped fresh parsley or basil
¼ cup leftover cooked pasta or vegetables
2 tablespoons oil
2 ounces mozzarella cheese, thinly sliced

Preheat broiler.

Beat eggs with grated cheese and herbs. Add leftovers and mix well.

Heat oil in a pan over medium flame. When oil is hot, pour egg mixture into pan and cook over medium-low heat until bottom is set, about 10 minutes.

Remove from stove, place mozzarella on top, and place under broiler until top is browned, about 5 minutes.

*SERVES 2*

**MAMMA SAYS:** My mother usually made this when she had a lot of leftovers, and believe me, it is tasty. You might even want to make extra broccoli or spinach with an eye toward using it here. In my own house, I never get to keep leftovers. When the family comes to dinner I cook large amounts, and then I wrap up any food that's left over for them to take home, especially on the holidays. My two grandsons Danny and Chris have their own apartments, and they look forward to eating Grandma's leftovers when they get home from work. I don't have to tell you how many times people of my generation were urged not to waste food.

# Spinach with Potatoes

2 potatoes, peeled and quartered
1 pound spinach, rinsed in several changes of water
1 clove garlic, minced
2 tablespoons grated Parmesan cheese
1 pinch salt
1 tablespoon olive oil

Place ½ cup water in a large pot and add quartered potatoes.

Layer spinach over potatoes. Sprinkle on garlic, cheese, and salt and drizzle on oil.

Cover tightly and simmer until potatoes are tender, 25 to 30 minutes.

*SERVES 4 TO 6*

My very young grandsons, Christopher (left) and Danny (right), at the wedding of their cousin Francine—she is the daughter of my sister Vi.

# Escarole with Potatoes

1 pound escarole
3 cloves garlic, sliced
1 tablespoon olive oil
3 potatoes, peeled and quartered
Salt

Parboil escarole for 2 to 3 minutes. Remove with a slotted spoon and set aside.

Sauté garlic in oil over medium heat.

Add escarole and potatoes to garlic and oil and salt to taste.

Cover and cook over medium heat until potatoes are soft, 15 to 20 minutes.

*SERVES 4 TO 6*

❧ **MAMMA SAYS:** My grandsons Danny and Christopher love this recipe. You will too.

# Eggplant Parmigiana

1 eggplant, about 1½ pounds
2 eggs
½ cup flour
½ cup olive oil or vegetable oil
2 cups tomato sauce (see pages 107–109)
½ cup grated Parmesan cheese
¾ cup cubed mozzarella cheese

Preheat oven to 400 degrees.

Cut eggplant into ⅛-inch-thick slices and set aside.

Beat eggs, whisking in enough of the flour to make a thick batter.

Pour oil into a heavy skillet. Oil should reach about ¾ inch from top of skillet. Heat oil over medium flame until very hot. Drop a bit of batter in to test it: the oil should boil around the batter.

Dip eggplant slices into batter, then place in oil, being sure not to crowd the pan. Turn and cook until both sides are golden. Drain on paper towels.

Place eggplant slices in a medium-size baking pan. Spread ¼ cup sauce, ¼ of the grated cheese, and ¼ of the mozzarella over eggplant. Continue layering until all ingredients have been used, ending with sauce, Parmesan, and mozzarella.

Bake until mozzarella is melted and has a golden brown top, 15 to 20 minutes.

*SERVES 4 TO 6*

᪣ **MAMMA SAYS:** This is a frequent request from the grandchildren.

# Giambotta

1 red onion
1 red bell pepper, seeded and cut into strips
1 green bell pepper, seeded and cut into strips
1 yellow bell pepper, seeded and cut into strips
2 plum tomatoes, seeded and diced
2 small eggplants, about 1 pound, diced
1 carrot, peeled and sliced in diagonal ½-inch-thick slices
1 large white onion, roughly chopped
1 zucchini, sliced in diagonal ½-inch-thick slices
3 cloves garlic, minced
1 bay leaf
1 teaspoon salt
½ teaspoon oregano or Italian seasoning
½ teaspoon crushed hot red pepper
½ cup olive oil or vegetable oil
2 tablespoons white wine vinegar
1 cup chopped basil
¼ cup chopped fresh parsley
Pepper

Combine all ingredients except ½ cup of the basil, the parsley, and the pepper in a large, flameproof casserole. Mix to combine.

Add 1 cup water, cover, and cook over medium heat, stirring occasionally, until vegetables are soft, about 30 minutes.

Remove and discard bay leaf. Sprinkle on remaining basil and parsley and season to taste with pepper.

*SERVES 4 TO 6*

# Roasted Peppers

5 red bell peppers
4 cloves garlic, sliced
2 tablespoons olive or vegetable oil

Preheat grill. Place peppers on grate over heated grill. Roast the peppers over low heat, turning them as they begin to blacken.

When peppers are charred (this will require grilling at least 5 minutes for each side), remove and place in a sealable plastic bag. When cool enough to handle, remove from bag. Peel off charred skins and core and seed the peppers. Cut the peppers into strips and place in a shallow dish. Add garlic and oil. Add extra oil to cover, if necessary.

*SERVES 4 TO 6*

**MAMMA SAYS:** These peppers are best served at room temperature.

# Stuffed Artichokes

1 cup bread crumbs
2 cups grated Parmesan cheese
3 cloves garlic, minced
1 pinch oregano
1 pinch paprika
Salt and pepper
½ cup plus 1 tablespoon olive oil
3 artichokes
2 tablespoons butter
½ cup milk
1 teaspoon cornstarch

Preheat oven to 375 degrees.

Combine bread crumbs, Parmesan cheese, and garlic. Mix in oregano and paprika and season to taste with salt and pepper. Mix in ½ cup oil.

Cut stems off artichokes and cut about 1 inch off tops. Trim points off leaves with kitchen shears. Steam artichokes by putting them in a pan with an inch of water over low heat. Cover and steam until soft, 10 minutes. Do not let water evaporate.

Stuff each leaf gently with a little of the bread crumb mixture and place artichokes in a baking dish. Drizzle remaining tablespoon oil over artichokes.

Bake for 30 minutes.

While artichokes are baking, make béchamel sauce. Melt butter in a small pot over medium heat. Add milk and whisk in cornstarch. Slowly bring to a boil, then lower heat to a simmer, stirring constantly, until sauce thickens to the consistency of sour cream.

Remove artichokes from oven and heat broiler. Pour béchamel sauce over artichokes and place artichokes under broiler until brown.

*SERVES 3*

↝ **MAMMA SAYS:** Stuffed artichokes are one of Al's favorite dishes.

Al walking his daughter Lisa down the aisle at her wedding to Jerry Murphy in St. Agnes Cathedral, Rockville Centre, Long Island.

# String Bean and Potato Salad

1 pound string beans
3 potatoes
1 red onion, sliced
⅔ cup olive oil
⅓ cup red wine vinegar
Salt and pepper

Trim string beans, put in steamer basket, and steam until tender. Set aside.

Put potatoes in a large pot of water and boil until tender, about 20 minutes. Set aside.

When vegetables have reached room temperature, slice potatoes and combine with onion and string beans.

Whisk together oil and vinegar. Pour enough over vegetables to moisten them. Season to taste with salt and pepper.

Refrigerate at least 1 hour before serving. You may want to moisten the salad with a little extra vinaigrette right before serving.

*SERVES 4*

◈ **MAMMA SAYS:** This is an easy side dish that goes well with meat, fish, and poultry.

# French-Cut String Beans

1 pound string beans
¼ cup olive oil
5 tablespoons tomato sauce (see pages 107–109)
1 teaspoon oregano
1 clove garlic, minced
¼ cup grated Parmesan or Romano cheese
Salt and pepper

Trim beans and cut French-style (lengthwise). Place sliced beans in a heavy skillet. Add ¼ cup water, oil, tomato sauce, oregano, garlic, and grated cheese. Season to taste with salt and pepper.

Cover skillet tightly and cook over medium-low heat for about 20 minutes, until beans are tender but still slightly firm.

*SERVES 4*

ᴥ **MAMMA SAYS:** Yet another easy one, and fast too. In the winter, when fresh string beans aren't available, you can use frozen cut string beans, which makes it even faster.

# Stuffed Zucchini

4 zucchini, whole
¼ pound ground beef
¼ cup grated Parmesan or Romano cheese
½ cup Italian bread crumbs
1 clove garlic, minced
2 tablespoons olive oil
Salt and pepper
Olive oil

Preheat broiler.

Wash zucchini and boil for 5 minutes. Drain and let cool.

When zucchini are cool enough to handle, cut off tops and cut them in half lengthwise. Scoop out pulp and mix with beef, cheese, Italian bread crumbs, garlic, and oil.

Cook beef mixture over medium heat, stirring occasionally, until meat is browned, 3 to 4 minutes. Season stuffing to taste with salt and pepper and stuff each zucchini half with the mixture.

Brush a baking pan with olive oil. Place zucchini stuffed side up in pan and dot with butter or drizzle with oil. Place under broiler until stuffing browns lightly.

*SERVES 4 TO 6*

# Stuffed Peppers

6 bell peppers, red or green
1 pound ground beef
1 cup cooked rice
1 clove garlic, minced
2 tablespoons chopped fresh parsley
1 teaspoon salt
1 teaspoon pepper
2 tablespoons grated Parmesan or Romano cheese

Preheat oven to 325 degrees.

Remove tops from peppers and reserve. Cut peppers in half and seed them. Boil for 5 minutes and let cool.

Combine all remaining ingredients. Fill a baking dish with 1 inch water. Stuff each pepper with rice mixture and place in baking dish. Replace pepper tops on stuffed peppers.

Bake until meat is brown, 40 to 45 minutes.

*SERVES 4 TO 6*

⌐ **MAMMA SAYS:** I like to combine different colored peppers in this dish. It looks pretty that way, and there is a subtle taste difference between the peppers as well.

# Artichoke Hearts and Mushrooms

1 cup bread crumbs
4 tablespoons grated Parmesan or Romano cheese
1 clove garlic, minced
5 tablespoons oil
Salt and pepper
2 (10-ounce) packages frozen artichoke hearts
12 ounces mushrooms, sliced

Preheat oven to 300 degrees.

Combine bread crumbs, grated cheese, garlic, and 1 tablespoon oil. Season to taste with salt and pepper.

Fill a deep baking dish with ⅛ inch water. Boil a small pan of water and blanch frozen artichoke hearts, about 3 minutes. Place layer of artichoke hearts in dish to cover bottom, then a layer of mushrooms, and sprinkle with bread crumbs to cover. Drizzle on a little oil. Repeat layers until all ingredients are used, ending with bread crumbs.

Cover and bake for 15 minutes. Uncover and bake a few more minutes to brown top.

*SERVES 4*

# Asparagus Pizzaiola

1 pound asparagus
1 cup tomato sauce (see pages 107–109)
1 clove garlic, minced
1 tablespoon grated Parmesan or Romano cheese
Salt and pepper
1 tablespoon olive oil
2 tablespoons chopped fresh basil

Preheat oven to 350 degrees.

Trim tough bottom stems from asparagus. Blanch asparagus by boiling for 3 minutes in a pot of water, then drain.

Place asparagus in a baking dish and top with tomato sauce and garlic. Sprinkle on grated cheese and season to taste with salt and pepper. Drizzle on olive oil.

Bake 25 minutes. Remove from oven and sprinkle with basil.

*SERVES 4*

# Fried Vegetables

1 small head cauliflower
1 small eggplant
1 red bell pepper, seeded
¼ cup cornstarch
¾ cup flour
½ teaspoon baking powder
1 egg
1 cup vegetable oil
Salt

Remove cauliflower florets and boil until just tender, about 5 minutes. Drain and set aside.

Cut eggplant in half lengthwise, then cut into ½-inch-thick slices.

Cut red pepper into strips.

Toss vegetables in cornstarch, shaking off excess.

Beat flour, baking powder, 1 cup water, and egg until smooth.

Heat oil in a large heavy skillet over medium flame. Dip a few vegetable pieces in batter and fry over medium flame until golden. Remove and drain on paper towels. Sprinkle with salt. Repeat with remaining vegetable pieces.

*SERVES 6 TO 8*

≈ **MAMMA SAYS:** Fried vegetables are a healthy first course or appetizer.

# Beer-Barrel Onion Rings

1½ cups beer
1 tablespoon baking powder
1 egg, beaten
1½ cups flour
Vegetable oil for deep frying
2 Spanish onions, thinly sliced
Salt

Whisk together beer, baking powder, and egg in a large bowl. Gradually whisk in flour.

Heat oil over high flame to 375 degrees.

Separate onions into rings. Dip a few rings into batter to coat, then fry until golden brown, about 30 seconds. Remove rings and drain on paper towels. Sprinkle with salt. Repeat with remaining onion rings.

*SERVES 4*

# DESSERTS

To me, a meal isn't complete without dessert. Even though sweets are getting bad press today, I'm convinced that we can finish meals with something flavorful that's not loaded with calories or fat.

Italians are known for their fruit tarts and light biscuits. Try fixing one of these, and I think you'll agree there is something splendid about a series of courses in a meal and about the admiring remarks from family and friends that follow a good dessert.

# Fresh Plum Tart

**CRUST**
8 tablespoons (1 stick) butter
1 cup sugar
1¼ cups flour
½ teaspoon salt
½ teaspoon cinnamon
¼ teaspoon baking powder
1 egg

**FILLING**
1 pound plums
1 tablespoon sugar
½ cup heavy cream
1 egg

Preheat oven to 375 degrees.

To make crust, cream butter and sugar in a large bowl. Add flour, salt, cinnamon, and baking powder. Mixture should be crumbly. Reserve ⅓ cup.

Add egg to remaining crumbs and mix until dough is smooth.

Press dough into an 11-inch tart pan with a removable bottom. Make sides slightly thicker than bottom.

To make filling, cut plums in half and remove pits. Arrange plums skin side up on top of crust. Sprinkle 1 tablespoon sugar over plums.

Bake tart for 15 minutes.

Beat cream with egg, pour over partially baked tart, and sprinkle with reserved crumbs from crust dough. Bake an additional 25 minutes or until filling is set.

*SERVES 8 TO 10*

ꝏ **MAMMA SAYS:** This recipe is a family favorite, and believe me, there are never any leftovers, except maybe a few crumbs.

# Cheesecake

**CRUST**

1½ cups crushed graham crackers

2 tablespoons sugar

3 tablespoons butter, softened

**FILLING**

1½ cups sugar

¼ cup flour

¼ teaspoon salt

2 pounds cream cheese, softened

6 eggs

8 ounces sour cream

1 tablespoon vanilla

Preheat oven to 350 degrees.

To make crust, in a medium bowl, combine graham crackers and sugar. Cut in butter. Knead until thoroughly combined. Press mixture firmly into the bottom of a 9-inch springform pan. Set aside.

To make filling, in a medium bowl, combine sugar, flour, and salt. In a large bowl, mix dry ingredients into cream cheese and combine thoroughly. Add one egg at a time to cream cheese mixture, slowly beating after each addition. Blend in sour cream and vanilla. Pour batter into prepared crust and bake until top is set, about 45 minutes.

Turn off oven and leave cake in warm oven, with door ajar, for 1 hour.

Refrigerate at least 1 hour before serving.

*SERVES 10*

᳁ **MAMMA SAYS:** A very good friend of mine makes this recipe in individual foil pans and gives these miniature cheesecakes as gifts on special occasions. In a pinch, you can use a store-bought graham cracker crust.

# Sour Cream Cake

2 cups cake flour
1 teaspoon baking powder
1 teaspoon baking soda
1 pinch salt
8 tablespoons (1 stick) butter or margarine
1¼ cups sugar
2 eggs
1 teaspoon vanilla
1 cup sour cream
½ cup chopped pecans
5 teaspoons cinnamon

Preheat oven to 350 degrees. Lightly butter an 8½ × 10-inch pan and set aside.

In a medium bowl, combine flour, baking powder, baking soda, and salt. In a large bowl, cream butter with 1 cup sugar, eggs, and vanilla. Alternately add small amounts of the combined dry ingredients and the sour cream, beating slowly after each addition.

In a small bowl, combine pecans, cinnamon, and remaining ¼ cup sugar.

Pour half of batter into buttered pan. Spread half of pecan mixture over batter, then top with remaining batter, and then top with remaining pecans.

Bake 35 to 40 minutes.

*SERVES 10 TO 12*

# Easter Pie

CRUST
½ cup sugar
3 tablespoons butter, softened
2 tablespoons Crisco
1 egg
1 teaspoon vanilla
½ cup flour

FILLING
2 pounds ricotta cheese
4 eggs
1 cup sugar
1 teaspoon cinnamon
1 teaspoon grated lemon zest
1 teaspoon grated orange zest

Preheat oven to 375 degrees.

To make crust, in a large bowl, cream sugar, butter, and Crisco. Mix in egg and vanilla and beat until smooth. Work in flour with hands. Cover and refrigerate for 30 minutes.

To prepare filling, place ricotta in large bowl. Mix in eggs, sugar, and cinnamon. Stir in lemon and orange zest.

Remove piecrust dough from refrigerator. Reserve one quarter of dough. On wax paper, roll out remaining dough to the size of an 8½-inch round cake pan and fit into pan, trimming off excess dough. Fill crust with ricotta mixture. Roll out remaining dough, slice into strips, and crisscross over filling to create a lattice topping.

Bake until crust is brown, about 1 hour.

Turn off oven and leave in warm oven, with door closed, for 30 minutes.

*SERVES 8 TO 10*

**MAMMA SAYS:** Many people in different parts of Italy enjoy Easter pie. Some add presoaked grain to make Easter grain pie. Either way you make it, this recipe brings back memories of long-ago Easters when families lived close and would visit each other for dessert.

Here's the family celebrating my brother Louis's birthday. From left to right: my son, Armand, with Al behind him, my mother, brother, sister-in-law, and my daughter Joanne.

# Sfingi (Ricotta Puffs)

2 eggs
¼ cup granulated sugar
½ cup ricotta cheese
1½ cups flour
2 teaspoons baking powder
¼ teaspoon cinnamon
½ cup milk
Vegetable oil for deep frying
2 tablespoons powdered sugar

In a large bowl, beat eggs and granulated sugar with electric mixer until light. Add ricotta and beat well. In a small bowl, combine flour, baking powder, and cinnamon and add to egg mixture alternately with milk. Blend well.

Heat oil over medium flame to 375 degrees. Drop dough into hot oil by tablespoons and fry until golden brown on each side, 2 to 3 minutes.

Remove and drain on paper towels. Sprinkle with powdered sugar.

*MAKES 2 DOZEN*

# Panzarotta

**PASTRY**
½ teaspoon yeast
2 cups flour
4 teaspoons granulated sugar
1 pinch salt
2 egg yolks
8 tablespoons (1 stick) butter or margarine

**FILLING**
½ pound ricotta cheese
¼ cup granulated sugar
1 teaspoon cinnamon

**FINISHING TOUCHES**
Vegetable oil for deep frying
2 tablespoons powdered sugar

To make pastry, dissolve yeast in 2½ ounces lukewarm water in a small bowl. Combine flour, salt, and granulated sugar in a large bowl, then stir in yeast liquid and yolks. Cut in butter.

To make filling, combine ricotta, granulated sugar, and cinnamon in a medium bowl and blend well.

Roll pastry dough out ¼ inch thick. Use a cookie cutter or juice glass to cut small circles.

Fill circles with ricotta mixture, fold over, and pinch edges with fork to seal.

Heat oil over medium flame to 375 degrees. Fry puffs a few at a time until golden. Remove to paper towels.

Sprinkle with powdered sugar.

*MAKES 2 TO 3 DOZEN*

⊰ **MAMMA SAYS:** My great-grandchildren love these and call them "little pies."

# Italian Biscotti

1 stick (½ cup) butter
¾ cup sugar
2 eggs
1½ teaspoons anise extract
2 cups plus 2 tablespoons flour
1½ teaspoons baking powder
¼ teaspoon salt
2 ounces chopped almonds

Preheat oven to 350 degrees. Butter a cookie sheet.

In a large bowl, cream ½ cup butter and sugar until fluffy. Beat in eggs until batter is smooth. Add anise extract and stir in flour, baking powder, salt, and almonds and mix well.

On a lightly floured board, form dough into two rolls, each about 16 inches long. Place dough rolls on prepared cookie sheet.

Bake until lightly golden, about 30 minutes.

Cool dough rolls for 5 minutes, then remove and place on clean board. Slice into ½-inch diagonal slices.

Lay slices on cut side on cookie sheet and return to oven for 3 minutes. Turn and bake another 3 minutes, until a little golden.

Cool and store in tightly covered container. These will keep for 2 weeks.

*MAKES 4 TO 5 DOZEN*

# Italian Nut Balls

¾ cup sugar
1 teaspoon salt
12 tablespoons (1½ sticks) butter, softened
2 egg yolks
½ teaspoon vanilla
½ teaspoon almond extract
½ teaspoon cinnamon
2 cups flour
1 cup finely chopped walnuts

Preheat oven to 350 degrees.

In a large bowl, combine all ingredients except walnuts and mix well.

Roll into balls 1 inch in diameter.

Spread chopped walnuts on a piece of wax paper. Roll balls in nuts until coated on all sides, then place on cookie sheets.

Bake until lightly golden, about 10 to 12 minutes.

*MAKES 3 TO 4 DOZEN*

# Wine Biscuits

4 cups flour
¾ cup sugar
4 teaspoons baking powder
1 teaspoon salt
1 cup Burgundy wine
1 cup vegetable oil

Preheat oven to 350 degrees.

In a large bowl, combine dry ingredients. Add wet ingredients and mix well.

Take a teaspoon or so of dough and use your hands to roll it out into a 6-inch rope. Pinch the two ends of the rope together and twist it several times. Place on cookie sheet. Repeat with remaining dough.

Bake until brown, 25 to 30 minutes.

*MAKES 3 TO 4 DOZEN*

# Meltaways

32 tablespoons (4 sticks) butter or margarine, softened
1 cup sugar
1 cup chopped nuts
3 cups flour

Preheat oven to 350 degrees.

In a large bowl, cream butter and sugar for 20 minutes until extremely light and fluffy. Stir in nuts and flour. Refrigerate for 30 minutes.

Remove from refrigerator and drop by ½ teaspoons about ½ inch apart onto ungreased cookie sheets.

Bake until edges are golden, 8 to 10 minutes.

*MAKES 3 TO 4 DOZEN*

❧ **MAMMA SAYS:** Make lots, because they'll go fast.

# Almond-Filled Pastry Crescents

**PASTRY**
1 cup flour
½ teaspoon salt
16 tablespoons (2 sticks) butter
4 tablespoons ice water

**FILLING**
1 (8-ounce) can almond paste
1 egg
2 tablespoons granulated sugar
⅓ cup ground almonds
⅔ cup powdered sugar

To make crust, in a large bowl, combine flour and salt and cut in butter. Sprinkle on ice water and mix until dough holds together. Shape into three balls of equal size. Wrap in wax paper, and refrigerate 1 hour.

Preheat oven to 400 degrees.

To make filling, put almond paste in bowl and break up. Beat in egg, sugar, and almonds until mixture is combined. Turn out onto a lightly floured surface. Flour your hands and shape into a ball. Divide into thirds.

Shape each ball into a rope ½ inch in diameter and 16 inches long. Cut into sixteen separate pieces, 1 inch each, and set aside.

Roll out one third of the pastry dough at a time to a thickness of ⅛ inch. This should be about 12 square inches. Trim uneven edges. Using ruler and pastry wheel, cut into sixteen 3-inch squares.

Place one piece of filling diagonally across each square. Roll dough around filling and curve into a crescent. Place 1 inch apart on ungreased cookie sheets. Repeat with remaining dough and filling.

Bake for 12 minutes, until golden brown, then sprinkle with powdered sugar.

*MAKES 4 DOZEN*

My husband Armand's birthday with granddaughters Lorraine (left) and Lisa (right), and their mother, Penny. I made Armand's favorite, strawberry shortcake.

# Mini Cherry Cheese Tarts

1½ pounds cream cheese
⅔ cup sugar
3 eggs
1 teaspoon vanilla
30 vanilla wafers
1 (21-ounce) can cherry pie filling

Preheat oven to 350 degrees.

In a large bowl, cream together cream cheese, sugar, eggs, and vanilla.

Place one wafer each in the bottom of thirty 2-inch foil cups. Fill with cheese mixture.

Place foil cups on cookie sheets and bake until golden, about 15 minutes.

When cooked, top each tart with 1 teaspoon cherry pie filling.

*MAKES 30*

ᴥ **MAMMA SAYS:** I've also made these with 2½-inch foil cups when I couldn't find 2-inch cups. I still used one wafer per cup and it worked fine and made twenty tarts. They were like small cheesecakes.

# German Cookies

4 cups flour
1 teaspoon salt
2 envelopes yeast
4 eggs
1 pint sour cream
l pound Crisco
1 cup powdered sugar

In a medium bowl, combine flour and salt. Mound the flour on a clean board and make a well in it. Place yeast, eggs, sour cream, and Crisco in well and cut with a knife until blended. Cover and refrigerate overnight.

The next day, preheat oven to 350 degrees.

Take a handful of dough at a time. Place on a floured board and roll and fold over three or four times, dusting lightly with powdered sugar each time.

Roll dough out to a thickness of ½ inch. Cut into 2-inch-wide strips, then cut strips into diamonds. Let rise 15 minutes before baking.

Place on a cookie sheet and bake until light gold, about 5 minutes (be sure to watch them carefully).

*MAKES 5 TO 6 DOZEN*

⊰ **MAMMA SAYS:** Most people like these because they're not too sweet. They're light and can be stored for some time (2 weeks).

# Pecan Tassies

**PASTRY**

6 ounces cream cheese, softened
16 tablespoons (2 sticks) butter or margarine, softened
2 cups flour

**TOPPING**

2 eggs
1½ cups brown sugar
1 tablespoon butter or margarine, softened
2 teaspoons vanilla
1 pinch salt
1⅓ cups ground pecans

Preheat oven to 375 degrees.

To make pastry, blend together cream cheese and butter in a large bowl. Stir in flour. Chill about 1 hour.

To make topping, cream eggs, brown sugar, butter, vanilla, and salt in a large bowl. Stir in nuts.

Shape pastry into balls 1 inch in diameter. Place in ungreased miniature muffin pans. Press dough evenly around sides and bottom of the muffin cups. Add enough topping to fill cups almost to the brim.

Bake until filling is set, about 30 minutes.

*MAKES 4 DOZEN*

# Crochette

**CRUST**
8 tablespoons (1 stick) butter or margarine
½ cup granulated sugar
2 egg yolks
2 cups flour
6 tablespoons ice water

**FILLING**
1 pound ricotta cheese
2 egg whites
6 tablespoons powdered sugar
2 teaspoons vanilla
¼ teaspoon grated lemon zest
⅛ cup miniature chocolate chips

Preheat oven to 400 degrees.

To make crust, cream butter and sugar in a large bowl. Add egg yolks. Add flour and blend well. Sprinkle on enough of the ice water to make a manageable dough. Knead dough on floured board until smooth. Roll out to ⅛-inch thickness. Reserve one third of rolled-out dough. Cut the remaining dough into twelve equal squares.

Butter a twelve-muffin tin. Line bottom and sides of each of the cups with a square.

To make filling, combine ricotta, egg whites, powdered sugar, vanilla, lemon zest, and chocolate chips in a large bowl. Fill muffin cups three-quarters full with filling.

Cut remaining dough into strips about ½ inch wide and crisscross over filling to create a lattice top.

Bake for 10 minutes, then reduce heat to 375 degrees and bake for 40 minutes or until browned on top.

*MAKES 1 DOZEN*

⊰ **MAMMA SAYS:** This is another Easter dessert that always has the family shouting, "More! More!"

# Scones

6 tablespoons butter or margarine, softened
3 teaspoons sugar
1 cup self-rising flour
¼ cup raisins
1 egg, beaten
Enough milk to make 1 cup when combined with egg

Preheat oven to 425 degrees.

Butter a cookie sheet and set aside.

In a large bowl, cream butter and sugar. Mix in flour and raisins. Add egg and milk, mixing well to combine with other ingredients. Knead a few times on lightly floured board, then roll out to ½ inch thick.

Cut out with doughnut cutter and place on prepared cookie sheet.

Bake until lightly browned, about 15 minutes.

*MAKES 1 DOZEN*

# Snack Muffins

¼ cup cocoa
1¼ cups flour
1 cup sugar
¾ teaspoon baking soda
½ teaspoon cinnamon
¼ teaspoon nutmeg
¼ teaspoon salt
¼ cup raisins
8 tablespoons (1 stick) butter or margarine, melted
¾ cup applesauce
1 egg

Preheat oven to 350 degrees.

In a large bowl, combine dry ingredients. Blend in wet ingredients and spoon into greased muffin tins.

Bake until lightly brown, about 20 minutes.

*MAKES 1 DOZEN*

It's Danny's birthday at my house in 1975. His brother, Christopher, is to the left and his sister Lorraine stands behind him. I made the chocolate cake.

# CANNING

My specialty in the kitchen is canning tomatoes. In fact, I have such a large demand from my family for my jarred tomatoes that I've never tried my hand at canning anything else. I put up about 200 jars at a time, and all my children and grandchildren come over and take some for themselves. Al always takes some jars to Washington with him.

Preparing fresh vegetables and fruits and other items and sealing them and putting them away for later use is thrifty, and those summer foods are comforting once the seasons have changed.

In preparing this book, I have been overwhelmed with recipes from fellow Americans from all over the country—and many of their recipes are heavily influenced by the foreign countries and cultures of their ancestors. What I loved about putting together recipes from other cooks and other families is that the ethnic backgrounds represented are as varied as the recipes.

Following are some ideas I hope you will try to use in your kitchens. My thanks and warm appreciation to all those who very generously became a part of this book.

Canning is fun, but it can be complicated. We all try

to keep clean kitchens, but hygiene, temperature control, timing, and storage conditions are even more important when you are canning. Also, the amount of time that canned goods need to be processed can vary according to altitude. *Always check with the agricultural extension agent in your area before attempting to can or preserve food.* Also, carefully read Lauren Malis's safety tips for canning using a pressure cooker on page 121.

When canning, always use new caps and lids designed specifically for that purpose. Never use lids a second time. Everything that comes into contact with the food, including caps and lids, must be sterilized, and the food itself should be cleaned thoroughly before you begin. This may sound obvious, but all items that are canned should be of the highest quality. Never let the hot jars touch tile or anything cool. Always set them down on a wooden cutting board or clean kitchen towel.

Finally, use your common sense. If you open a jar and get a whiff of something funny, or if there is any kind of mold growth on your canned products, or if they feel slimy, or if the lids cannot be closed tightly, discard them. *When in doubt, throw it out!* Even if your food doesn't look suspicious, as a further safeguard you can boil your food for 10 minutes before serving to destroy any toxins that may be present. Add an additional minute of boiling time for each 1,000 feet of altitude, starting at 1,000 feet above sea level.

# Mamma's Tomato Sauce I

My tomato sauce is the pivotal ingredient in just about all of my recipes.

I had the pleasure of attending a luncheon with Bernadette Castro and Libby Pataki at a restaurant not too long ago. Bernadette is the New York State parks commissioner and Libby is the wife of George Pataki, the governor of New York. The owner spotted me and asked if I wanted to visit his kitchen and taste the tomato sauce. I did and told him that it was really just okay. He asked, "It isn't as good as yours?" and I answered, "No." Sorry, I can't lie about it. My sauce is the best.

It's the best because it's plain: not too heavy, not too light, but just right. I usually cook the sauce a couple of hours before I put it in the jars. I put a piece of fresh basil in the bottom of each jar, so when you open a jar of my tomatoes you can smell the basil and also lightly taste it.

My tomato sauce is flexible too. You can sauté meat and add it to the sauce. Or you can do a sauté of onion and garlic and whatever other seasonings you like. What is great about this is that you can cook your pasta while you're whipping up the sauce, and in no time both are done at the same moment and all you have to do is add the cheese!

1 bushel plum tomatoes
Salt
2 bunches basil

Wash, trim, seed, and quarter tomatoes. Fill a juice machine three quarters of the way with tomatoes. Grind tomatoes until still slightly pulpy.

Pour the tomato sauce into a very large saucepan. Grind any remaining tomatoes and continue adding tomatoes to saucepan until it is at least three-quarters full.

Add salt to taste and bring to a boil. Continue boiling until puree is thickened to your liking.

With sauce still boiling, place a basil leaf in a hot, sterilized canning jar, prepared according to manufacturer's instructions, and fill with sauce. Seal immediately—again, following manufacturer's instructions—and place upside down in a box covered with black plastic so the jars cool very slowly. Repeat with remaining sauce.

When the jars have cooled for 2 to 3 days and are cold, check seals.

*MAKES 12 TO 14 QUARTS*

⊰ **MAMMA SAYS:** If you don't have a Vita Mix or other juice machine, see the Tomato Sauce II recipe that follows.

# Mamma's Tomato Sauce II

1 bushel plum tomatoes
Salt
2 bunches basil

Wash, trim, seed, and quarter tomatoes.

Place tomatoes in a large saucepan and bring to a boil. Simmer briskly, stirring occasionally, until they are soft, at least ½ to ¾ of an hour.

Ladle the hot tomatoes into an Italian sauce machine, which will separate the skin and any remaining seeds from the pulp. Follow machine instructions.

Pour the tomato sauce into a very large saucepan. Puree any remaining tomatoes and continue adding puree to saucepan until it is at least three-quarters full. Add salt to taste and bring to a boil. Continue boiling until sauce is thickened to your liking.

With sauce still boiling, place a basil leaf in a hot, sterilized canning jar, prepared according to manufacturer's instructions, and fill with sauce. Seal immediately—again, following manufacturer's instructions—and place upside down in a box covered with black plastic so the jars cool very slowly. Repeat with remaining sauce.

When the jars have cooled for 2 to 3 days and are cold, check seals.

*MAKES 12 TO 14 QUARTS*

᷾ **MAMMA SAYS:** You can purchase an Italian sauce machine in New York City's Little Italy or in gourmet kitchenware stores around the country.

# ANN ZAVALA

Ann Zavala, who now lives in California, has moved around the world with her husband and three daughters and has brought back dishes from all their travels. Ann learned to can from her grandmother, who eventually sold her preserves business to Smucker's.

The author of over thirty nonfiction and fiction books, Ann cans every year.

## Ann's Strawberries in Pineapple Juice

1 case strawberries
2 (46-ounce) cans pineapple juice

Wash, drain, and hull the strawberries. Quarter strawberries the long way. In a large saucepan, bring the pineapple juice to a boil.

Fill a hot, sterilized canning jar, prepared according to manufacturer's instructions, with berries, leaving the jar clear from the rim upward. Ladle boiling pineapple juice over the fruit. Seal according to manufacturer's instructions. Repeat with remaining fruit.

Process jars in a boiling water bath for 10 minutes. Remove jars and check seals.

*MAKES 15 TO 20 ½-PINT JARS*

◈ **ANN SAYS:** Strawberry jam is wonderful on toast or over ice cream, but during the winter, when the best fruits available are apples, oranges, and bananas, we long for the unadulterated taste of warm strawberries fresh from the back hill. These look like red jewels, and while they aren't quite as good as absolutely fresh berries, they are definitely a cut above super-sweet strawberry jam. You can substitute raspberry or grape juice for the pineapple juice if you wish.

# Ann's Peaches in Apple Juice

4 quarts apple juice
11 pounds peaches

In a large pot, bring apple juice to a boil.

In a wide pot, bring water to a boil. Add peaches and boil for 1 minute, then remove to a colander. Run cold water over the peaches.

When peaches are cool enough to handle, peel them, halve them, and remove the pits.

Fill a hot, sterilized pint-size canning jar, prepared according to manufacturer's instructions, with peach halves, filling the jar almost to the top. Pour boiling apple juice over the halves. Seal according to manufacturer's instructions. Repeat with remaining fruit.

Process jars in a boiling water bath for 10 minutes. Remove jars and check seals.

*MAKES 9 PINTS*

ANN SAYS: My husband and I are trying to cut down on sugar as we age, so I've been experimenting with various ways to can without sugar. Two years ago I tried canning peaches with no sugar at all, but the results were disappointing—they had the taste and texture of wet straw. Last year, I experimented with peaches in various fruit juices. I liked peaches in apple juice the best, with pineapple juice running a close second. Raspberry juice was fine and gave the peaches a soft red color, but the two flavors didn't complement each other as much as I had expected. If you're feeling frisky, look around and try something different on at least a couple of your jars of fruit.

# Ann's Spiced Peach Preserves

15 pounds peaches
¾ cup sugar
½ cup lemon juice
2 tablespoons whole cloves
1 tablespoon ground cinnamon
1 cup brandy

In a large pot filled with water, boil peaches for 1 minute, then remove to a colander. Run cold water over the peaches.

When peaches are cool enough to handle, peel them, halve them, and remove the pits.

Put the peaches in a large, heavy pot. Add sugar, adjusting to taste. Add lemon juice, cloves, and cinnamon.

Bring the peaches to a boil. If the mixture looks too thick, add a bit of water, but be cautious since the peaches will get much more liquid as they cook. Cook the boiling preserves over low heat, stirring constantly. Cook them for about 10 minutes for chunky preserves, a little longer for smooth preserves.

When preserves are cooked, add 1 cup brandy and stir well. Turn the heat down so that the mixture is at a brisk simmer. Keep it simmering while you fill all jars.

Fill a hot, sterilized ½-pint-size canning jar, prepared according to manufacturer's instructions, with preserves, leaving about ½-inch headspace. Seal according to

manufacturer's instructions. Repeat with remaining preserves.

Process the jars in a boiling water bath for 10 minutes.
Remove jars and check seals.

*MAKES 4 ½ PINTS*

ᴂ **ANN SAYS:** When my mother was a young girl living on
the farm in Bern, Idaho, evening meals were invariably
fresh bread, honey, and milk, or fresh bread, peach
preserves, and milk. This is also good mixed into vanilla
ice cream.

# Ann's Lemon-Tomato Preserves

10 pounds tomatoes
4 lemons
Sugar

Bring a large pot of water to a boil. Boil tomatoes for 30
seconds, drain until cool enough to touch, then peel. If the
cores are thick, core them too. Place the tomatoes in a
nonreactive pot over very low heat.

Meanwhile, thinly slice lemons. Add the lemon slices to
the tomatoes. Add about 1 cup of sugar for every 2 cups of
tomato mixture, adjusting for your taste.

Cook the mixture until it turns from bright red to
browner red, thickens, and the lemons are translucent,
about 10 to 15 minutes.

Fill a hot, sterilized ½-pint-size canning jar, prepared
according to manufacturer's instructions, leaving ½-inch
headspace. Seal according to manufacturer's instructions.
Repeat with remaining preserves.

Process jars in boiling water bath for 10 minutes. Remove jars and check seals.

*MAKES ABOUT 1 DOZEN ½-PINT JARS*

ANN SAYS: When my mother was running Leone's Swiss Kitchens, we'd spend most of our summer at the custom cannery in Nampa, Idaho, making up jars that would be included in the Neiman Marcus Christmas boxes. The owner of the custom cannery loved my mother's lemon-tomato preserves and would hang around the big steam kettles and watch as the ingredients were added. He was trying to figure out the recipe, but no matter how many times he tried to make it, it never tasted the same as my mother's. He pestered her unmercifully for the "secret" ingredient that made her preserves so much better than his own, but she never told him. Instead, she'd bring in ten-pound bags of sugar already mixed with the secret ingredient, and add that to the tomatoes and lemons. The secret ingredient made the sugar just slightly brown, and the poor man never did figure out what my mother was adding to that mix. I'm not going to tell you either. These preserves are as close as you can get to the real recipe.

Our family often eats meat the old Swiss way, with a sweet item and a sour item as side dishes. This preserve is the sweet that is served with roast beef or plain roast pork. Add some mashed potatoes with plenty of butter and cream, marinated green beans, and maybe a green salad and you've got a wonderful meal.

# Ann's Pickled Peppers

30 peppers of various colors
5 pounds canning (noniodized) salt
3 quarts distilled white vinegar

½ cup to 2 cups sugar, depending on taste
4 tablespoons mustard seed
6 cloves garlic
1 tablespoon white pepper

Trim and seed peppers and cut them into strips. Place pepper strips in a nonreactive pot. Add 4 quarts of water (preferably filtered) and 1 cup salt. Continue to add water and salt in those proportions until peppers are completely covered. Stir to distribute evenly.

Cover the pot and let rest in a cool place for 12 to 18 hours.

Thoroughly rinse the peppers under cold water.

In a large pot, bring vinegar, 6 cups water, ½ cup sugar, mustard seed, garlic, and white pepper to a boil.

Loosely pack a hot, sterilized pint-size canning jar, prepared according to manufacturer's instructions, with peppers. Do not allow the peppers to extend above the shoulder of the bottle. Ladle boiling vinegar mixture over peppers, leaving only ½ inch air space in jar. Seal following manufacturer's instructions. Repeat with remaining peppers.

Process in a boiling water bath for 15 minutes.

Remove jars and check seals.

*MAKES 4 PINTS*

ANN SAYS: We use these pickled peppers in Greek salads, as a complement to the Kalamata olives and the feta cheese. They're also good added to plain pinto beans that have been cooked with an onion and hot peppers. Cut up some cheese and fresh onion, dice the peppers, and sprinkle everything over the beans and you've got a good meal.

# Ann's Mélange à Trois

Various soft fruits
Brown sugar
Juice
Raisins
Whole cloves
Cinnamon
Apple cider vinegar
Brandy

Wash, peel, and cut up any fruit you have lying around. Discard bruised sections.

Place fruit in a nonreactive pot. Add about 1 cup brown sugar for every 6 to 8 cups of fruit. For every 8 or so cups of fruit, add about 2 cups juice, 2 cups raisins, 2 tablespoons whole cloves, 2 tablespoons cinnamon, and 1 cup apple cider vinegar. Use about 1 cup brandy.

Bring the fruit mixture to a boil and boil rapidly for 5 minutes, stirring constantly. Reduce the heat to a simmer. Keep it simmering while you fill all jars.

Fill a hot, sterilized canning jar, prepared according to manufacturer's instructions, with the fruit mixture, leaving ½-inch headspace at the top. Seal following manufacturer's instructions. Repeat with remaining fruit mixture.

Process jars in a boiling water bath for 10 minutes. Remove jars and check seals.

*A 6-QUART POTFUL OF COOKED FRUITS WILL YIELD APPROXIMATELY 8 TO 10 ½-PINT JARS*

⌐ **ANN SAYS:** I tend to overbuy on fruits, so I'm always opening a drawer in the refrigerator and realizing that there are several pounds of fruit just ready to turn to mush if I don't use them right away. This isn't really a recipe, more of a guideline for using over-the-hill but not quite dead fruit.

We use this as a fruit side dish with a hot chicken or beef curry, or tandoori chicken. I've also been experimenting with using the mix in my own brand of lassi. I whip ⅓ cup plain yogurt, ⅓ cup buttermilk, ⅓ cup mélange à trois, ⅓ cup fruit juice, and a few tablespoons of rose water in a blender.

# Ann's Apricot-Pineapple Marmalade

4 cups pitted, halved apricots, unpeeled
2 (20-ounce) cans pineapple chunks, packed in natural juice
1½ cups sugar
5 to 15 whole cloves
2 tablespoons lemon juice

Put apricots, pineapple chunks, pineapple juice, and sugar in a large pot and bring to a boil, stirring constantly.

Once the mixture is boiling, reduce heat to medium and continue stirring constantly while sprinkling in the cloves. Add the lemon juice. Boil for a few more minutes until the apricots lose their shape, about 10 minutes.

Fill a hot, sterilized small (½-pint or less) canning jar, prepared according to manufacturer's instructions, with marmalade. Seal following manufacturer's instructions. Repeat with remaining marmalade.

Process jars in a boiling water bath for 10 minutes.
Remove jars and check seals.

*MAKES 3 OR 4 PINTS*

**ANN SAYS:** If you want to eliminate the sugar entirely, cook the fruit, pineapple chunks, cloves, and juice until the mixture is reduced by one third to one half to concentrate the natural sugars.

# SANDRA MIESEL

Sandra Miesel of Indianapolis, Indiana, has been a professional writer for 25 years. She holds graduate degrees in biochemistry and medieval history. Her studies were splendid preparation for writing, editing, and analyzing science fiction.

Presently, Sandra is a religion journalist who sometimes writes articles about cooking. She is married and has three grown children.

## Sandra's Apple-Herb Jelly

2 cups bottled apple juice or pasteurized cider
1 cup minced fresh lemon verbena leaves
1 cup minced fresh pineapple sage leaves
3½ cups sugar
1 pinch salt
2 tablespoons apple cider vinegar or white balsamic vinegar
3 ounces liquid pectin

In a saucepan, bring apple juice to a boil, pour over herbs, and let steep for 15 minutes. Strain through a coffee filter into a large bowl. There should be 1½ cups liquid.

Stir liquid with sugar, salt, and vinegar and place in a nonreactive pot. Bring to a rolling boil. Add the pectin, return to a rolling boil, and boil exactly 1 minute.

Remove from heat, skim off foam, and ladle into a hot, sterilized canning jar, prepared according to manufacturer's instructions. Seal following manufacturer's instructions. Repeat with remaining jelly.

Process in a boiling water bath for 10 minutes. Remove jars and check seals.

Allow to set 1 to 2 days before using.

*MAKES 4 ½-PINT JARS*

⌛ **SANDRA SAYS:** If you wish, substitute ½ cup minced fresh sage leaves and ½ cup minced fresh thyme leaves, or 1½ cups minced fresh mint leaves, or ½ cup minced fresh savory leaves plus ½ cup minced fresh thyme leaves for the lemon verbena and pineapple sage leaves.

# LAUREN MALIS

Lauren Malis is a part-time restaurant/food consultant for event planning and restaurateurs and also a professionally trained chef. She is currently at work on her second cookbook.

She and her mother, Dolores Malis—who are Italian-Lithuanian—have been canning vegetables together for as long as they can remember.

Lauren explains that all vegetables, with the exception of pickled beets and tomatoes, must be processed in a pressure cooker to guarantee safety. A pressure cooker allows water inside to boil and form steam; the steam that is trapped inside the canner builds pressure and seals the food jars.

Many people are afraid of using pressure cookers but do not have to be if they follow carefully the directions that come with their cooker and do not attempt to try any shortcuts. Lauren stresses that it is important to check the cooker before using by looking at all openings to make sure they are clean and unclogged. Check the pressure gauge; it should remain accurate if the cooker is properly cared for. If for some reason the gauge is off, have it checked by the manufacturer. She also stresses two important things before canning with a pressure cooker: *Follow the manufacturer's directions and always watch the cooker while it is in use.* Because directions for each pressure cooker can differ, you *must* read the directions for your own cooker.

Lauren says she generally goes by the following rules when using her own canner, and shares them with you so that you can get a general sense of what goes into pressure cooking. *However, these are not a substitute for following the directions on your own cooker.*

Place the cooker on your heat source, with a rack on the bottom of the cooker. Fill with about two inches of water, or whatever the manufacturer recommends. When you place your food jars in the cooker, they should be arranged so that they are not touching each other or the sides of the cooker. Fasten the cover securely after the jars are placed in the cooker.

The vent must be left open and enough time allowed so that steam will push out all the air that is in the cooker—this should be about 8 minutes, and you will see a steady flow of steam. Close the vent and keep an eye on the gauge. Most foods are processed at 10 pounds, but check each of the recipes Lauren has included for the right amount. Begin timing when the proper pressure is reached. Do not leave the cooker unattended. A slight change in pressure can mean that it is not processing correctly. And always be aware of how long the food has been processing—a minute here or there can make all the difference in the world.

When the process time is finished, take the cooker off the burner if you are using an electric stove or cooktop. (Be very careful lifting your cooker). Just turn off the heat if it is a gas stove. Wait until the pressure drops to zero before opening the lid of your cooker. At zero open the vent to let out any steam that is remaining (this is very important). After the steam is out, open the cover in the direction that is *away* from you.

Lift the food jars carefully out of the pressure cooker onto towels in a dry place. Check seals after 12 hours. Label all the jars with the date of processing and store in a cool, dry, and dark place.

## READ THIS INFORMATION CAREFULLY

Lauren says it is very important to look for the following before eating any food that you have canned:

- Bubbles inside the jar
- Mold
- Food that has turned dark or an unusual color
- Cloudy liquid
- Any leakage around seal
- Shriveled food
- Bulging lids
- A fermented, musty, or other unusual odor after opening the jar
- Squirting liquid (like that from a champagne bottle) when the jar is opened.

DO NOT USE THE FOOD IF YOU SEE THESE SIGNS. THROW THE FOOD OUT IN A PLACE WHERE NO ONE—INCLUDING CHILDREN, PETS, OR WILD ANIMALS—CAN GET AT IT.

There are two methods for canning most garden vegetables—the raw-pack method or the hot-pack method. Lauren says the hot-pack method is, in general, the best one to use when canning vegetables. It essentially means that you precook the food, allowing for a tighter pack and requiring fewer jars. When you use this method, you bring food to a boil, simmer it for a few minutes, then pack it loosely into hot jars along with any required hot liquid.

The raw-pack method is for low-density foods (such as tomatoes), which hold their shape better if they are packed raw. The food is placed in the jar while it is raw, and packed firmly but not crushed. After packing, boiling water is added to those foods that require additional fluid. The jars are then placed in hot, not boiling, water. (Since the jars are still cold, they might break if placed in hot water.)

Lauren suggests that all vegetables be very fresh and ripe and preferably canned the day they are picked. You may keep them in the refrigerator overnight, but they should be processed the next day. When canning food, leave some room between the lid and the top of the vegetable or fruit. This is called headspace and usually ranges from half of an inch to an inch. The recipes that follow indicate the amount of head room to leave. Lauren also explains with each recipe the amount of vegetables you will need to fill a one-quart jar. It's up to you to decide how much you want to can!

# Lauren's Canned Asparagus

Please note: 2½ to 3½ pounds of asparagus will yield approximately 1 quart of canned asparagus.

In a large pot, bring water to a boil. Stir in salt.
Meanwhile, wash and trim asparagus. Peel rough ends.
Loosely pack asparagus upright in a hot, sterilized quart-size canning jar, prepared according to manufacturer's instructions. Pour in boiling salted water, leaving ½ inch headspace, and seal following manufacturer's instructions. Repeat with remaining asparagus.

Pressure process at 10 pounds (240 degrees) for 30 minutes.

Remove jars and check seals.

# Lauren's Canned Lima Beans

Please note: 3 to 5 pounds of lima beans will yield approximately 1 quart of canned limas.

In a large pot, bring water to a boil. Stir in salt.

Shell beans and boil until tender. Immediately ladle beans into a hot, sterilized quart-size canning jar, prepared according to manufacturer's instructions. Pour in boiling salted water, leaving 1 inch headspace. Seal following manufacturer's instructions. Repeat with remaining beans.

Pressure process for 1 hour and 45 minutes at 10 pounds (240 degrees).

Remove jars and check seals.

# Lauren's Canned String Beans

Please note: 1½ to 2½ pounds of green beans will yield approximately 1 quart of canned string beans.

In a large pot, bring water to a boil.

Wash beans and trim ends. (Or, if you wish, cut beans French-style or in 1-inch pieces.)

Fill a hot, sterilized quart-size canning jar, prepared according to manufacturer's instructions, as tightly as you can. Add 1 teaspoon salt. Pour in boiling water, leaving

½-inch headspace. Seal following manufacturer's instructions. Repeat with remaining beans.

Pressure process at 10 pounds (240 degrees) for 30 minutes.

Remove jars and check seals.

# Lauren's Canned Corn

Please note: 1 bushel of corn yields 12 to 20 pints of canned corn (depending on the size of the ears of corn).

Bring water to a boil.

Husk corn and wash thoroughly to remove all silk. Cut kernels from the cob.

Fill a hot, sterilized quart-size canning jar, prepared according to manufacturer's instructions with corn kernels, leaving 1 inch headspace. Do not pack too tight. Add 1 teaspoon salt. Pour in boiling water, which should cover corn well. Seal following manufacturer's instructions. Repeat with remaining corn.

Pressure process at 10 pounds (240 degrees) for 1 hour and 30 minutes.

Remove jars and check seals.

✲ **LAUREN SAYS:** In August, when white corn is available from farms, take advantage of the abundance because you will enjoy the summer taste in the cold winter months.

# Lauren's Canned Eggplant

Please note: 2 to 4 pounds of eggplant will yield
approximately 1 quart of canned eggplant.

Wash and peel eggplant. Cut into slices or cubes.

Place the eggplant in a roasting pan. Sprinkle with salt
and cover with cold water. Soak for 1 hour.

Bring water to a boil.

Drain eggplant and pat dry with paper towels.

Loosely pack a hot, sterilized quart-size canning jar,
prepared according to manufacturer's instructions, with
eggplant. Add boiling water, leaving 1 inch headspace.
Seal following manufacturer's instructions. Repeat with
remaining eggplant.

Pressure process at 10 pounds (240 degrees) for 40
minutes.

Remove jars and check seals.

₰ **LAUREN SAYS:** This wonderful and healthy vegetable
does lose its looks when canned, but it is great to have to
mix with other vegetables or with sauce or cheese.

# Lauren's Canned Summer Squash

Please note: 2 pounds of squash will yield approximately
1 quart of canned squash.

Bring water to a boil.

Wash squash and trim ends, but do not peel. Cut into
slices or cubes.

Pack squash tightly into a hot, sterilized canning jar,
prepared according to manufacturer's instructions, leaving

1 inch headspace. Pour in boiling water, leaving ½-inch headspace. Water should cover squash. Add 1 teaspoon salt. Seal following manufacturer's instructions. Repeat with remaining squash.

Pressure process at 10 pounds (240 degrees) for 30 minutes.

Remove jars and check seals.

# Lauren's Canned Winter Squash

Please note: 2 pounds of squash will yield approximately 1 quart of canned squash.

Wash and peel squash. Remove seeds and pulp and discard. Cut squash into 1-inch cubes.

Place squash in a saucepan and cover with water. Bring to a boil and cook until soft. Drain squash and reserve hot liquid.

Fill a hot, sterilized quart-size canning jar, prepared according to manufacturer's instructions, with squash. Pour in the boiling water that the squash was cooked in, leaving ½-inch headspace. Add 1 teaspoon salt. Seal following manufacturer's instructions. Repeat with remaining squash.

Pressure process at 10 pounds (240 degrees) for 1 hour and 30 minutes.

Remove jars and check seals.

&? **LAUREN SAYS:** For a puree, you can put the squash through a food mill or strainer, then simmer over low heat, stirring constantly. Pack hot with no added liquid or salt, leaving ½-inch head space. Follow processing instructions for squash cubes.

# JOAN MEHRO TAYLOR

Joan Mehro Taylor of Minnesota offers her recipe for bread-and-butter pickles, and another for dill pickles from her former mother-in-law, Vivian White. Although both Joan and Vivian married into a Scandinavian family, their recipes reflect their Alsatian and Czech backgrounds.

## Joan's Bread-and-Butter Pickles

1 gallon thinly sliced cucumbers
½ cup noniodized salt
3 onions, thinly sliced
4½ cups sugar
4 teaspoons white mustard seed
1½ teaspoons turmeric
1¼ teaspoons celery seed
5 cups vinegar

Place sliced cucumbers in large pan. Sprinkle with ¼ cup salt. Layer onion slices over cucumbers and sprinkle with remaining salt. Cover with chopped ice or ice cubes and let stand 1 hour. Drain well. Taste a cucumber slice. If it seems much too salty, soak the cucumbers and onions in clean, cold water for 10 minutes and drain again. Mix thoroughly.

Bring sugar, mustard seed, turmeric, celery seed, and vinegar to a boil in a large nonreactive pot. Add cucumber and onion mixture and boil 5 minutes. Fill a hot, sterilized pint-size jar, prepared according to manufacturer's instructions, with pickles. Leave about an inch of head space. Seal with sterilized lids following manufacturer's instructions. Repeat with remaining pickles.

When cool, check seals.

*MAKES 7 TO 8 PINTS*

# Vivian's Dill Pickles

16 sprigs dill
8 stalks celery
18 pounds small pickling cucumbers
1 quart vinegar
1 cup noniodized salt
16 cloves garlic

Rinse dill well and let drain. Clean celery and scrub cucumbers.

In a large pot, add vinegar and salt to 3 quarts water and bring to a boil.

Fill a hot, sterilized canning jar with 2 sprigs dill, 2 cloves garlic, and 1 stalk celery. Tightly pack in cucumbers. Pour boiling vinegar liquid into jars, leaving ½-inch headspace. Seal following manufacturer's instructions.

When cool, check seals.

*MAKES 8 QUARTS*

# BEVERLY "BEVY" JAEGERS

Beverly "Bevy" Jaegers of Sappington, Missouri, has been canning for more than 30 years. She started when she was raising six children on a limited budget.

Bevy is the former food editor of a St. Louis newspaper. She has contributed recipes to the Home Shopping Network's newsletter and is currently at work on a cookbook. She has also published several non–food-related books.

If her recipes have a distinct Southern flavor, there is a reason for that: Bevy is a descendant of General Robert E. Lee.

## Bevy's Ozark Delight Bread-and-Butter Pickles

5 pounds cucumbers
4 white onions, thickly sliced
6 cups dark brown sugar
3 pints apple cider vinegar
1 teaspoon powdered alum
3 teaspoons celery seed
1 tablespoon mustard seed
3 teaspoons nasturtium seed or dill seed
2 green bell peppers, seeded and coarsely chopped
1 red bell pepper, seeded and coarsely chopped
2 drops green food coloring
1 drop yellow food coloring
1 cinnamon stick

Peel and slice cucumbers. Place cucumber slices and onions, separated into rings, in a large bowl. Cover with lightly salted water. Let soak overnight in a covered bowl.

After cucumbers are put to soak, bring sugar, vinegar, alum, celery seed, mustard seed, and nasturtium seed to a boil in a large nonreactive pot. Add peppers, boil for 10 minutes, then let that sit overnight as well.

The next day, in a 6-quart pot, bring vinegar-pepper mixture to a boil, drain the cucumbers and onions and add to mixture. Cook over medium heat for 5 minutes. Add food coloring.

Break cinnamon stick into six pieces. Place a piece of cinnamon stick in the bottom of a hot, sterilized pint-size canning jar, prepared according to manufacturer's instructions. Use a slotted spoon to fill with pickles. Pack down and pour in hot vinegar-spice liquid, leaving as little air space as possible. Seal following manufacturer's instructions. Repeat with remaining pickles and liquid.

When cool, check seals.

*MAKES 6 PINTS, PLUS A CUPFUL FOR THE COOK*

⊰ **BEVY SAYS:** These pickles are great with any hot or cold meat dish.

# Bevy's Little Italy Olive-Oil Pickles

12 to 15 small, hard cucumbers (peeled or unpeeled),
    thinly sliced
2 red onions, thinly sliced
¼ cup salt
1 clove garlic
1 cup white vinegar

1¼ teaspoons powdered alum
⅔ cup extra-virgin olive oil
2 teaspoons white mustard seed
1 tablespoon celery seed
1 teaspoon cumin seed
1 tablespoon dill seed
1 teaspoon mixed Italian herbs

Layer cucumber and onion slices in a large mixing bowl. Salt and place heavy plate on top. Let stand overnight.

Crush garlic and place in vinegar. Let stand overnight.

The next day, drain all liquid from cucumber and onion slices. Combine vinegar, 1 cup water, and alum in a small bowl and pour over drained cucumbers and onion slices and toss to coat. Let stand 4 to 5 hours.

Drain all liquid from cucumbers and onions, reserving 1 cup of the garlic vinegar. Remove garlic from vinegar with a fork or slotted spoon and discard. Mix reserved liquid with olive oil. Toss cucumber and onion slices with seeds and herbs. Pack tightly into hot, sterilized pint-size canning jars, prepared according to manufacturer's instructions. Pour olive oil mixture over pickles to fill jars completely. Seal following manufacturer's instructions. Repeat with remaining pickles.

When cool, check seals.

Let stand 3 weeks to cure before using.

*MAKES 4 TO 5 PINTS*

☙ **BEVY SAYS:** If you find you need more vinegar and water mixture to cover the pickles completely, mix ⅓ cup olive oil with ⅔ cup vinegar and water. Do not add additional alum.

# Bevy's Santa Claus Relish

1 cup sugar
1½ cups apple cider vinegar
2 tablespoons mustard seed
1 tablespoon celery seed
¾ tablespoon salt
6 green bell peppers, cored, seeded, and chopped
6 red bell peppers, cored, seeded, and chopped
4 stalks celery, chopped
2 large sweet onions, chopped

Combine sugar, vinegar, mustard seed, celery seed, and salt with ½ cup water in a deep, nonreactive pot. Bring to a boil, then add chopped peppers, celery, and onions and reduce heat to moderate and simmer 7 minutes, stirring gently.

Using a slotted spoon, fill a hot, sterilized pint-size canning jar, prepared according to manufacturer's instructions. Seal following manufacturer's instructions. Repeat with remaining relish.

When cool, check seals.

*MAKES 6 PINTS*

⊰ **BEVY SAYS:** This relish works wonderfully as an addition to tuna, chicken, turkey, or potato salad, deviled eggs, or even a garden salad.

# Bevy's Missouri Corn Relish

1 cup apple cider vinegar
½ teaspoon mustard seed
½ teaspoon turmeric
½ teaspoon celery seed
½ teaspoon cumin seed
1½ cups sugar
2 teaspoons salt
½ teaspoon pepper
3 tomatoes, peeled and quartered
4 cups fresh corn kernels
3 red onions, coarsely chopped
1 red bell pepper, cored, seeded, and chopped
1 green bell pepper, cored, seeded, and chopped

Combine vinegar, mustard seed, turmeric, celery seed, cumin seed, sugar, salt, and pepper in a deep, nonreactive pot. Bring to a boil, then add tomatoes, corn, onions, and bell peppers.

Cook, uncovered, over moderate heat and stirring frequently, for 5 minutes, then reduce to a simmer and cook, covered, until corn is very tender, about 30 minutes.

Fill a hot, sterilized pint-size canning jar, prepared according to manufacturer's instructions, with relish. Seal following manufacturer's instructions. Repeat with remaining relish.

When cool, check seals.

Allow jars to stand in a cool, dark place for at least 2 weeks before using.

*MAKES 3 TO 4 PINTS*

⊰ **BEVY SAYS:** If fresh corn is not available, drained canned or rinsed frozen corn makes an acceptable substitute.

# INDEX

meat (*cont.*)
  spinach and sausage pie, 63
  stew, 43
  veal and mushroom oreganata, 46
  veal kidneys, 47
  veal rollatini, 45
  veal steak, 44
  meatballs, Italian, 52
  meatball soup, instant, 26
  meatloaf, 51
  mélange à trois, Ann's, 116–17
  meltaways, 95
  Miesel, Sandra, 119–20
    apple-herb jelly, 119–20
  mini cherry cheese tarts, 98
  Missouri corn relish, Bevy's, 136
  muffins, snack, 103
  mushroom(s):
    and artichoke hearts, 78
    baked rice with peas and, 17
    and veal oreganata, 46

nut(s):
  almond-filled pastry crescents, 96–97
  Italian balls, 93
  meltaways, 95
  pecan tassies, 100

olive-oil pickles, Bevy's Little Italy, 133–34
onion(s):
  beer-barrel rings, 81
  chicken with peppers and, 37
Ozark delight bread-and-butter pickles, Bevy's, 132–33

panzarotta, 91
parmigiana, eggplant, 69
pasta, 1–13
  with beans, 12
  with broccoli, 7
  fast dish, 8
  grandsons', 9
  lasagna, 11
  Mamma D'Amato's homemade sauce I, 3

  Mamma D'Amato's homemade sauce II, 4
  puttanesca, 6
  quick linguine with clams and shrimp, 10
  spaghettini with artichokes, 5
  stuffed shells, 13
pastry crescents, almond-filled, 96–97
peaches in apple juice, Ann's, 111–12
peach preserves, Ann's spiced, 112–13
peas, baked rice with mushrooms and, 17
pecan tassies, 100
pepper(s):
  Ann's pickled, 114–15
  Bevy's Missouri corn relish, 136
  Bevy's Santa Claus relish, 135
  chicken with onions and, 37
  pork chops, 48
  roasted, 71
  sausage and potatoes, 64
  stuffed, 77
pickles:
  Ann's pickled peppers, 114–15
  Bevy's Little Italy olive-oil, 133–34
  Bevy's Ozark delight bread-and-butter, 132–33
  Joan's bread-and-butter, 130–31
  Vivian's dill, 131
pies:
  Easter, 88–89
  spinach and sausage, 63
pineapple-apricot marmalade, Ann's, 117–18
pineapple juice, Ann's strawberries in, 110–11
pizzaiola, asparagus, 79
plum tart, fresh, 85
pork:
  chow mein à la Mamma D'Amato, 42
  Italian meatballs, 52
  pepper chops, 48
potato(es):
  escarole with, 68